MW00414532

Bunny
Jan. 2013

LIFE IN THE PSALMS

OTHER PETER JEFFERY TITLES

In addition to *Life in the Psalms* Solid Ground is honored to be able to offer the following titles from the same author:

CHAINS OF GRACE: *The Peter Jeffery Story*

"Spirit-anointed preachers who are simple, clear, biblically faithful and who aim at conversion is the need of the hour. May our God raise up many more men with Peter's gifts and graces to herald the mercies of Peter's Savior." —**Pastor Steve Martin**

"I commend this easy-to-read journey of a man who found Jesus Christ and wants to tell others about him. Peter Jeffery has done that and still is doing it through this book and others. Thrown into the bargain are real questions on true preaching, what it is, and true conversions which are clearly and simply answered and explained." —**Neville Rees**

OPENING UP EPHESIANS FOR THE YOUNG

"When I hear the name Peter Jeffery, I immediately think of the author who is known for his ability to put profound biblical truth in readable, understandable and memorable language. That ability is on display again in this volume as Mr. Jeffery explains both the sublime doctrine and the practical instruction of the apostle Paul in his letter to the Ephesians.

The young people for whom this volume is intended will find Peter Jeffery's clear and perceptive style much to their liking. They are certain to come away from their reading of it with a greater understanding of the glory of salvation and with firm determination to live more for the glory of the One who graciously provided it." —**Roger Ellsworth**

SEEKING GOD: *Do You Really Want to Know God?*

"We have used Peter Jeffery's *Seeking God* for many years to show unbelievers of all ages how to 'seek the Lord while He may be found'. It has proved most effective in special Sunday School classes, as a popular item on our tract rack with visitors and in believers' personal distribution to their friends. *Seeking God* shows you *how* to seek God, cautions you how *not* to seek God and encourages you as to *why* it all matters. Unlike so much fluff today, this is older, wiser, biblical counsel from a veteran 'obstetrician of souls.'" —**Steve Martin**

LIFE IN THE PSALMS

Reflections on
the Greatest Devotional Book in the World

Peter Jeffery

Solid Ground Christian Books
Birmingham, Alabama USA

Solid Ground Christian Books
PO Box 660132
Vestavia Hills AL 35266
205-443-0311
mike.sgcb@gmail.com
www.solid-ground-books.com

LIFE IN THE PSALMS
Reflections on the Greatest Devotional Book in the World

Peter Jeffery

© 2011 Peter Jeffery. All Rights Reserved.

Cover design by Borgo Design
Contact them at borgogirl@bellsouth.net

ISBN- 978-159925-318-3

TABLE OF CONTENTS

INTRODUCTION

Christians love the psalms. These 150 gems are a delight to any believer because they are the joys and sorrows of God's people of the past that exactly mirror our present experiences. The psalmists were not theorizing about God but recording their experiences for the enrichment of believers in all generations. The ups and downs of life are here and that is why Christians love them. We can identify with them and they may encourage or rebuke us but they never leave us empty.

The psalmists all demonstrate the reality of life with God. Sometimes this life is known in all its delights, but sometimes it is lost sight of and has to be sought again. Not that we ever lose it but we can lose the reality of it. There is nothing nominal or formal about the psalmist's religion. Everywhere it vibrates with life. It is this life in all its glorious hues that we look at in this book.

Life is not all plain sailing and spiritual life is no different. The essential mark of a Christian is that he has spiritual life. It is not natural to any of us and comes as a gift of God in regeneration. Spiritual life is to know and love God. It enables us to understand and respond to the word of God. Often it is a sheer delight but sometimes it is a battle. It can bring us into situations that are painful and would be avoided if we were not

Christians, but as believers there is no avoiding some difficulties. Psalm 59 records such a situation. The problems were real but David is still able to end the psalm with confidence in God—'O my strength. I will sing praise to you; you, O God, are my fortress, my loving God.'

It has been over fifty years since the Lord had mercy upon me and drew me to Christ. The book of Psalms has been used by God to minister to me more than any other book, and has been useful to me in ministering to others as well. In this brief book I invite you to a taste of the greatest devotional book in the world. It is my sincere hope and prayer that you will come to love it and the Lord who has given it for the good of our souls.

Peter Jeffery
Port Talbot, Wales
May 2010

Psalm One

A HAPPY LIFE

God wants his people to be happy, therefore the Bible has a lot to say about happiness. In the Psalms 'blessed' means happy, so Psalm 1 is telling us what is necessary to make a person happy.
Happiness is a very flimsy thing. For most folk it depends upon circumstances. If a man wins the lottery happiness is guaranteed, but if he loses his job or his health declines then happiness will not be possible. By this standard, happiness is a fleeting allusion, always dancing in and out of our lives and never constant or permanent. In contrast, the Bible tells us that God's way is a truly happy one. This happiness is not an end in itself; rather it is a by-product of something more basic and more important.

The first psalm tells us clearly what makes a man happy. The psalmist says that happiness depends upon our relationship to God.

THE WRONG WAY

The happy man is someone who does not do certain things. The world does not like negatives especially in the area of moral behavior and thinking. It finds them restrictive. The negative is frowned upon as being a miserable way to live. But the Bible is

9

always using negatives to make its point. For instance, in the Ten Commandments God could easily have said that we must be honest. Instead he said, 'You shall not steal.' He could have said that we must respect our marriage vows, but instead he said, 'You shall not commit adultery.' By using the negative the truth is emphasized and no one can misunderstand.

The happy man 'does not walk in the counsel of the wicked or stand in the way of sinners or sit in the seat of mockers' (Psalm 1:1).

Not walking in the counsel of the wicked means that he does not take his standards and behavioral pattern from the current whim of the world. Trendy TV producers and godless newspaper editors are not allowed to mould his thinking. This being true he does not stand or sit, make himself at home, with the godless attitudes of the broad way.

The person consumed with admiration for the broad way will never be happy because the happiness it offers is one massive delusion. The world will never know real happiness simply because it is preoccupied with it. Its so-called happiness is therefore always shallow and artificial, always dependent upon circumstances. It is not difficult to prove this. Just consider the sort of people the TV and newspapers always hold up to us as ones to be admired and if possible to be imitated. The so called stars are so happy that they cannot exist without drugs, excessive drinking and three or four marriages. That's the type of happiness we are better off without

THE RIGHT WAY

What is it that makes a man happy? It is to experience God's way of salvation and live to please God. Psalm 1 puts it like this: 'his delight is in the law of the Lord, and on his law he meditates day and night' (v. 2).

To many people nothing could be more dreary and boring than this. To a man on the broad way such a conclusion is inevitable. Such concepts are foreign to him but at one time they were foreign to us all. No one naturally lives like this. This pattern of behavior is found only on the other side of the narrow gate.

Here is a man who takes his standards, thinking and attitudes from the revealed will of God. This means he has a standard that does not change. This is exactly the opposite of the world whose standards are changing all the time. Also he has a standard outside of himself and therefore not dictated by his own weaknesses and prejudices. This gives an authority and purpose to his life.

Such a man takes God seriously. He does not play at religion. Christianity is not a hobby to him but the centre of his life. It is possible to be in church every Sunday and still take your standards from the world. It is also possible to call yourself a Christian and not delight in the law of the Lord. These things are possible if a man has no real relationship with God. His religion is as empty as another man's life of drink and sex.

HAPPINESS IS...

1. Having your greatest problem dealt with.
Life is full of problems and no one avoids them. But the greatest problem by far is the one of our own personal sin and guilt. Unless this is dealt with it will take us to hell for eternity.

All people are by nature great optimists when it comes to God. They think that in the end everything will be all right. They know they are not as good as they should be, but there are plenty of people far worse than them so, they think, God is bound to accept them. It is only when a man begins to listen to what God says in the Bible that this false optimism disappears. He sees there how seriously God takes sin and this shakes him. What use is it being as good as the next man if that man is going to hell?

A veneer of happiness can be maintained by ignoring what God says. After all, judgment and hell are considered to be old-fashioned and outdated beliefs. But the trouble is that death is not old-fashioned and it is coming to us all. Death, no matter what men may say, makes judgment and hell very real. The happy man is the one who knows that death holds no terror for him because his sin has been dealt with once and for all by the Lord Jesus Christ.

2. Having a peace that no one can take away.
The peace God gives us is not dependent upon circumstances but upon the eternal worth of what Christ has done for us. It is the peace that does not disappear when life gets rough. Jesus promised us that what he gives us, thieves will never be able to steal and moth and rust never be able to destroy.
God's way is the way of life more abundant. This does not mean that it is littered with gadgets and material possessions but filled with the reality of God. No wonder the man who knows this is happy.

3. Having a guaranteed future.
For most people the future means from now until the grave. For the Christian it means from now and for all eternity.

Guarantees are notoriously unreliable things. We are urged to read the small print to be sure of the terms. Very few things are guaranteed for life and when things do go wrong it is not always easy to claim on your guarantee. Perhaps it has run out or the particular part you need is not covered. We have all known this. But God's guarantee has no small print, there is no time limit and everything is covered. It depends upon the unfailing love of God in Christ. Those on God's way are saved for eternity. Heaven is guaranteed them and there are no catches. It is true happiness to know this.

Some people want to dismiss Christianity as 'pie in the sky when you die', and choose instead to live out the false illusion and flimsy happiness of being in this world without God. But being without God is also to be without hope and that is the most terrible of all situations.

The Christian's happiness is not obtained only when he reaches heaven but the moment he steps through the narrow gate onto God's way.

Psalm Three

A TROUBLED LIFE

If Psalm 1 speaks of a happy life and is one of the great ups in our experience, then Psalm 3 is one of the downs and shows us David in great trouble.

Psalm 3 comes out of what was one of the saddest experiences in David's life. He had known many trials and disappointments but none like this. His son Absalom was rebelling against him and seeking the throne for himself. David had known much opposition in his life, particularly from King Saul, but this was different—this was his own son. We learn of the incident in 2 Samuel 15, and there we read in verse 30 that this man of God wept bitterly as he contemplated this most severe of all opposition. If this were not enough to cope with, David was told that Ahithophel had joined forces with Absalom. This man had been one of his closest friends and had served well as David's chief adviser. The king's high regard for Ahithophel is shown us in 2 Samuel 16:23, where we are told that 'The advice Ahithophel gave was like that of one who enquires of God.' This opposition was a bitter pill for David to swallow. He laments,

Even my close friend, whom I trusted,
he who shared my bread,
has lifted up his heel against me
(Ps. 41:9).

Troubles rarely come singly. Often they crowd upon one another and seem to compete to pull us down. Son and best friend act against this man of God. It is the experience of most of us that what we can take bravely from strangers becomes a bitter blow when inflicted by loved ones. David laments:

If an enemy were insulting me, I could endure it;
if a foe were raising himself against me,
I could hide from him.
But it is you, a man like myself,
my companion, my close friend,
with whom I once enjoyed sweet fellowship
as we walked with the throng at the house of God
(Ps. 55:12-14).

Spurgeon, in his *Treasury of David*, comments on these verses: 'Reproaches from those who have been intimate with us, and trusted by us, cut us to the quick; and they are usually so well acquainted with our peculiar weaknesses that they know how to touch us where we are most sensitive, and to speak so as to do us most damage. The slanders of an avowed antagonist are seldom so mean and dastardly as those of a traitor, and the absence of the elements of ingratitude and treachery renders them less hard to bear.'

DAVID'S REACTION

How are we to react as Christians in a situation like this? That will depend on how we see the hand of God in our problems. David's reaction to this particular problem was to run away (2 Sam. 15:14). He made no defense because he saw no hope of victory. Why did this man of action give in so easily? Was it because he was disillusioned and depressed? Was it because he was old and tired? Was it because it was his son and friend who were conspiring against him and he had no stomach for such a fight? No, it was none of these things. David knew that all these events were part of God's judgment upon him because of his sin with Bathsheba. God had warned him: 'The sword shall never depart from your house, because you despised me and took the wife of Uriah the Hittite to be your own.' This is what the Lord says: 'Out of your own household I am going to bring calamity upon you. Before your very eyes I will take your wives and give them to one who is close to you, and he will lie with your wives in broad daylight. You did it in secret, but I will do this thing in broad daylight before all Israel' (2 Sam. 12:10-12). Absalom was the one out of his own household, and Ahithophel was Bathsheba's grandfather. There was no doubt in David's mind why this was happening, so he did not resist what he saw as God's judgment.

Here we see a lovely spirit in David. Early in his life the same attitude was obvious when he was suffering for righteousness; now here it is again when he is suffering because of his own sin. As a martyr hounded by Saul, we can see the fruits of meekness, patience and confidence in God as he refused to take revenge on Saul on the two occasions he had his enemy at his mercy. But here David is not sinned against, but the sinner. His sin has found him out, and he submissively bows his head and accepts the consequences.

There are times when as Christians we have to suffer for the sake of righteousness, but there are other times when our trials and problems are a direct result of our own sin. It is true that there is no eternal condemnation for the Christian, but that does not mean that God allows us to get away with sin. Sin brings consequences. It did for David and it will for us. What we are to learn from David is how to react when we know that God is dealing with us because of our sin.

David's reaction was twofold: he wept and he prayed. His weeping was not the tears of self-pity as, sadly, are often the case when Christians are caught in their sin. The picture in 2 Samuel 15:30 reveals to us that these were tears of repentance: 'But David continued up the Mount of Olives, weeping as he went; his head was covered and he was barefoot.' A. W. Pink says of this, 'Throughout he is to be viewed as the humble penitent. God's rebuke was heavy upon him, and therefore did he humble himself beneath His mighty hand. Hence it is that we here see him giving outward expression to his self-abasement and grief for his sins, and for the miseries which he had brought upon himself, his family, and his people. Suitable tokens of his godly sorrow were these, for the covering of his head was a symbol of self-condemnation, while his walking barefooted betokened his mourning.' (*The Life of David*, Baker, 1985, volume 2, p. 118)

REPENTANCE

True repentance will always lead to prayer, and some believe that it was in the midst of his tears of repentance upon the Mount of Olives that David wrote Psalm 3. To feel the consequences of sin without repentance will turn us in upon ourselves in despair and self-pity. This produces all sorts of different reactions in a Christian. We may feel bitter and critical of God. David could have thought that God was dealing too harshly with him. After all, the child who was the product of his sin with Bathsheba was dead. Surely that was enough punishment. And after the Bathsheba incident his repentance, as seen in Psalm 51, had been real and deep. Why were the consequences of that sin still arising? What believer has not experienced such thoughts at some time or other? Bitterness follows such a response and then, instead of repentance, we feel hard done by. It is God who is wrong, not us.

It may be that we feel confused. If the Bible says that there is no condemnation to those who are in Christ, and if we are told that God puts our sins behind his back and remembers them no more, and if Scripture teaches that the blood of Jesus Christ cleanses us from all sin—why is it that the consequences of sin are so real, so heavy and so painful?

God opposes sin with a pure, holy hatred, and he wants us to see it as he sees it. Sin is open rebellion against the character and law of God. It is a refusal to accept the authority and rule of God. It is bowing to the lordship of Satan and rejecting the lordship of Christ. In many ways sin in a believer is far worse than sin in an unbeliever.

There is no excuse for it because we are dead to sin (Rom. 6:11), we have been freed from sin's power (Rom. 6:6) and sin is no longer our master (Rom. 6:14). When the Christian sins, he is offering himself to sin to be used to promote wickedness (Rom. 6:13). That is terrible and we need to see it as such. It is true that there are no eternal consequences for the sin of the believer. Jesus took care of all that on the cross. But because God loves us, he will not allow us to get away with sin. If he did we would never take it as seriously as God does. We should hate sin because God hates it, but often we do not. So God shows us the evil of this rebellion by letting us feel here and now something of the consequences of sin. It is part of the teaching process that is seeking little by little to conform us to the mind of God.

Yet another reaction when we see the reality of our own sin is to stop praying. We feel too unworthy, too unclean, to come into the presence of God. The devil is eager to strengthen this feeling and keep us away from the Lord.

PRAYER

If David felt any of these reactions, thankfully by the time he came to the Mount of Olives he was past them and he came humbly to God in prayer, with no confusion and no bitterness. The prayer of Psalm 3 is a beautiful reminder to us of how to approach God when we are suffering as a consequence of our own sin.

Firstly in verse 1, he faces up to the gravity of the situation. He is not deluding himself. There is no virtue in pretending everything is fine, when clearly it is not. We are not to whistle in the dark or pour out pious platitudes about the love of God. David, facing reality, spells out for us in verses 2-4 three important truths.

What the world says

The world says God will not help him. It is easy to understand this belief. After all, David is guilty. What is happening to him is only what God said would happen. Why should God help?

What the Christian knows

God does chastise his people, but only because he loves them. As Christians we should never forget this. Our dealings with

God are always on the basis of grace, not merit. We deserve nothing, but God is always a shield around us. This is true even when our difficulties are of our own making.

What the Christian does

He prays; he cries to his God. We are never to despair as if there were no hope. Whether we are innocent or guilty in a particular situation, prayer is always to be our reaction.

The rest of the psalm is an example of true, believing prayer. Here we see, in this terrible situation, David's confidence, trust, courage, dependence and assurance. 'He answers me,' says David in complete confidence (v. 4). This us not because we are good or bad but because our God is a loving Father and we are his children. Such confidence will produce the trust of verse 5. Worry and despair rob us of many things, including sleep, but the person trusting God sleeps in peace. The hymn-writer is correct when he wrote,

> *Oh, what peace we often forfeit,*
> *Oh, what needless pain we bear,*
> *All because we do not carry*
> *Everything to God in prayer!*

We really do get ourselves into a terrible mess if we refuse to trust God.

If confidence produces trust, then it is surely true that both produce courage. Thus David is able to say, 'I will not fear.' It is possible to pray and feel as miserable and fearful afterwards as we did before. This is because prayer is much more than just words. Prayer without a confidence and trust in God will not produce the courage that David exhibits in this psalm. When all three are present we shall know the sense of dependence David had upon God. 'Arise, O Lord! Deliver me, O my God', are the words of a man who had stopped trusting his own efforts. His eyes are now upon God. The whole sorry mess he was in came about because he took his eyes off God and let his lusts and desires rule him.

The whole process of believing prayer results in the assurance that 'From the Lord comes deliverance' (v. 8). God was chastising David, but this did not go on forever. Eventually his enemies were routed and David was given back the throne. The lesson was needed. It was a hard time for this man of God but it was necessary. It always is.

Psalm Sixteen

A SAFE LIFE

Psalm 16 has been called the Golden Psalm or David's Jewel and these titles are not extravagant. Both Peter and Paul quote from it in the Acts in reference to the Lord Jesus Christ (Acts 2:24-31, Acts 13:35-38). The contexts of both those passages in Acts are the risen Jesus. The Apostles delighted in the fact of the resurrection. What greater confirmation can there be of the Christian gospel? Here our hope and assurance find a solid foundation. Obviously David when he wrote the Psalm knew nothing of the great truth of the resurrection, but he knew what it was to be kept safe by God (verse 1), also he had a marvelous appreciation of all that the Lord had done for him—'Lord, you have assigned to me my portion and my cup; you have made my lot secure. The boundary lines have fallen for me in pleasant places; surely I have a delightful inheritance.' (verses 5-6).

Safety and security rested for David in the one who had made known to him the path of life (verse 11). The Psalmist is on a mountaintop of spiritual bliss. He gains bright views of a glorious future, and he is assured of life, resurrection and immortality. All this does not mean he is living in some fantasy land where everything is easy and free of problems. If he has to ask God to keep him safe (verse 1), he knows of troubles that could overwhelm him. He may well have a delightful inheritance but that does not mean he cannot be shaken (verse 8). It is not his delightful inheritance that keeps him safe, but the fact that he has 'set the Lord always before me' (verse 8).

There are basic lessons here for all Christians to learn.

There may be some Christians who object that being victors in Christ sounds great, but it is not working for them. All they seem to experience is one defeat after another. One reason for this may be a lack of trust in God. There are many believers who want everything tied up neatly and tidily before they will do anything. Unlike Peter on the Sea of Galilee (Matt. 14:28-31), they would never even get out of the boat. It is easy to criticize Peter for becoming fearful, but at least he had the faith to trust Jesus and get out of the boat and walk on the water.

Another reason is the failure to realize that God does not give us all the victory after one battle. We remember God's promise in Exodus 23:29-30: 'But I will not drive them out in a single year, because the land would become desolate and the wild animals too numerous for you. Little by little I will drive them out before you, until you have increased enough to take possession of the land.' We need to remember the words, 'little by little'.

Why did the Lord not deal with the Canaanites before Israel arrived? Why did they have to fight? Why does God not make it impossible for us to sin? Why do we have to face the continuous struggle against the world, the flesh and the devil? There are many answers to these questions and one is that 'little by little' keeps us in a state of constant dependence upon God. The battles are not so much to defeat the enemy, but to deal with our arrogance and self-confidence and to teach us more and more to lean upon the Lord.

God never promises us complete victory over sin all at once; therefore we should not be surprised by the battles. If Israel was not to be discouraged by their slow progress in the Promised Land, neither must we be discouraged if victory is not ours at once. We must not think that slowness means that victory will never come. Growth in grace is not instantaneous, like new birth; it is gradual and takes time. This is not to encourage spiritual indifference and laziness. Our business is to get into the battle, to fight and obey and trust the Lord for victory. It may be 'little by little' but it is sure: 'No one will be able to stand up against you all the days of your life. As I was with Moses, so I will be with you; I will never leave you nor forsake you' (Joshua 1:5).

THE RIGHT PATH

Safety means being on the right path. This path David calls the path of life as distinct from the path that leads to death and hell. As you read the Bible you find that the writers are all concerned with what they call the way or the path. By this they mean the path a man is taking through life—his beliefs, behavior, attitudes and concerns. All these make up the path. Because of this it may be thought that there are a multitude of ways a person can take through life, but the fact is there are only two. Jesus said in Matthew 7:13-14 that there is either the broad way or the narrow way.

Narrow does not mean narrow minded or restrictive. It is true that the narrow path will not allow certain things on it—sexual immorality, drunkenness, selfishness, pride or jealousy. Some might say it sounds very restrictive; on the contrary, David who was on the narrow path said it was full of good and pleasant things (verses 5-6).

This path is not one on which we are born. It is one made known to us by the Lord. It is the path that leads to life, to God, and to heaven. Put very simply, the way is Jesus. He said that he was the only way to God (John 14:6). It is not an easy path and there are many problems to be confronted.

The characteristics of this path are repentance, love, obedience and holiness. It is narrow in that sin still takes pot shots at us and the Christian fails often, but all this is outweighed with what David calls the eternal pleasures found on it (verse 11).

Men and women have always sought pleasure. There is nothing wrong with that, it becomes wrong when pleasure becomes a god. Then it becomes the aim in life and everything else is sacrificed to achieving it. Paul says in 2 Timothy 3:4 that one of the marks of sin dominating a life is that the person becomes a lover of pleasure rather than a lover of God. Pleasure is not wrong. It is where you find the pleasure that can be wrong. Today's teenagers find it in their pop music and video games, dads in their car or sports and mums in their bingo or shopping. These become gods in their lives. They may be alright in their place. The trouble is that they do not stay in their place.

The Psalmist probably saw the equivalent in his day, but he had discovered pleasures that last, eternal pleasures at God's right hand.

Do you as a Christian know these pleasures?

We are saved by grace and have known something of God's mercies and blessings. We can read in Scripture of our rich spiritual inheritance, but we are stagnant and indolent. Instead of going on with Christ we have become comfortable and nothing is allowed to disturb our spiritual slackness. No effort is made to mortify our lusts and no serious energy put into seeking holiness. Our Christian life just drifts, with no direction and no purpose. Our problem is that we are satisfied with being saved. It may be objected, 'What is wrong with that?' Everything! It is wrong to be satisfied with being a babe in Christ and never wanting to grow. It is like a man being saved from drowning, pulled out of the sea, brought to the safety of the beach, and then spending the rest of his life making sandcastles. To these Christians God says, 'How long will you be slack and not claim all the blessings I have for you in Christ?'

Other Christians mourn about the moral and spiritual state of the nation, but the truth is that they are happy as they are. They are content with believing the right doctrines but knowing nothing of the power of the Holy Spirit. Correct doctrine, though crucial, is no substitute for the presence and power of God.

A safe life is great but it is not an end in itself. It should lead on to a full enjoyment of God.

Psalm Nineteen

A THRILLING LIFE

It is not difficult to see the thrill in David's heart as he writes this psalm.

In Psalm 19 David is confronted with the glory and majesty of God. Verses 1-6 describe all creation in beautiful language, testifying to the goodness and glory of God. Then in verses 7-11 his attention changes to the Scriptures and his heart is lifted as he contemplates the richness of revealed truth to his soul.

He sees God and thinks about God's requirements of him. This is thrilling because the ways of God are not daunting but enlivening to his heart. They are precious and sweet and so rewarding when kept by us.

But no man can see and appreciate the greatness of God without at the same time being made aware of his own sin.

In verses 12-13 David is forced to look at his own heart and he does not like what he sees there. Hidden faults and willful sins are a solemn reminder of a sinful nature that never leaves us alone.

Have you found that the closer you draw to God the more aware and concerned you become of your sin? This is not unusual and is not necessarily bad. It certainly should not be depressing. God shows us our sinful hearts in order to create in us a greater desire for holiness and a more urgent longing to be pleasing to our Lord and Savior.

If we are complacent about our sin it is because we have lost sight of the majesty of God. The clearer we see the Lord, the greater will be the desire in us to be rid of all that displeases him. There will be a longing to be blameless and innocent, and the prayer of verse 14 will dominate our desires and ambitions. There is no greater ambition than to be as holy as it is possible for a sinner to be.

In verse 10 David makes a thrilling discovery and it is one that runs contrary to human experience. To most people gold is one of the most precious things in the world. Gold is the power behind paper money. Men have built their lives on seeking it, others have died for it and some have even killed for it. But David had discovered something more precious than gold and that is the word and will of God.

To an unbeliever this would be a most ridiculous statement. To such a person the word of God would not come into his one hundred most precious list. The Christian however agrees with the Psalmist. In Psalm 119 we read, 'The law from your mouth is more precious to me than thousands of pieces of silver and gold' (verse 72), and in the same psalm in verse 127, 'I love your commands more than gold, more than pure gold.'

Why is the word and will of God more precious than gold? The answer is given in verse 11, 'By them is your servant warned; in keeping them there is great reward.'

God's word warns us about our true state before the Lord and this produces the sort of prayer of verses 12 and 13. Our errors, hidden faults, and willful sins are all revealed to us as we read the scriptures. The Bible is like a mirror. As we look into it we see ourselves as we really are. Nothing is hidden, and nothing is passed over. In this the Bible is unique for nothing else is a true reflection of our nature. Certainly our own hearts and minds tend to give us a rosy picture of ourselves. We may admit we are not perfect but as we compare ourselves to others we feel quite satisfied with our performance. We find it easy to agree with Romans 3:23 'for all have sinned', but we put the emphasis on the ALL not the SIN. We then hide in a crowd of general accusations and excuse ourselves by saying that we are no different to anyone else.

It is as we look closely and seriously at the word of God we see that we are not as good as we thought we are. Our life is full of errors, hidden faults and willful sins. And these are not harmless embellishments because they seek to rule us. Such awareness throws the soul on God for mercy.

The person who has been brought to see these things is rich indeed. From conviction of sin, grace is opened up to him and there is no more precious thing in all the world than to know the grace of God.

Grace is not some vague notion but is a definite act on the part of God. It is God doing for the sinner what no one else could do and what the sinner could never earn or merit. Grace is a unique work of God and it is a completed work. It could never be improved upon. The grace of God in the gospel is as perfect as anything can be. Even God himself could not improve upon the grace he has shown us in Jesus Christ.

It is the love of God that makes Calvary possible, but it is the holiness of God that makes it necessary. Grace flows out of divine love and fully satisfies God's holiness. When grace begins its work it never forgets the absolute holiness of God, therefore it has to provide for the sinner a salvation that does not gloss over or minimize the effect of sin. There must be no short-cut salvation; no salvation on the cheap; no theoretical dealing with sin. God's holiness cannot be deceived or satisfied with such things. The objective of grace is not merely to make sinners accept God, but to make it possible for the holy God to accept sinners.

The warning leads to the reward. The reward of salvation is forgiveness of sins and acceptance with God. These are riches we will never lose. They are protected and guaranteed by God himself. How much better is this than gold.

Psalm Twenty-Two

A LIFE IN CHRIST

Charles Spurgeon said of this Psalm, 'This is beyond all others the Psalm of the cross. David and his afflictions may be here in a very modified sense, but he who sees Jesus will probably neither see nor care to see David'.

Spurgeon was spot on in this assessment and merely to read Psalm 22 will confirm this.

Verse 1. Jesus uttered these words on the cross.

Verses 7-8. Here are words found on the lips of the enemies of Jesus at Calvary.

Verse 16. A very clear description of crucifixion.

Verse 18. Amazingly fulfilled to the letter as recorded in Matthew 27:35.

Here we see not vague, general statements but absolute detail. The question arises how could David write these things one thousand years before Jesus was born? The only answer is that

God was speaking through him. God wants us to see that the cross was all part of the divine plan of salvation.

The Christian delights in this. His love for Jesus is strengthened by such Old Testament passages. The life of the believer, whether in Biblical times or more modern times is a life wrapped up in Jesus Christ. He would have no life at all apart from what the Savior did for him on the cross. The life we have in Christ is one that comes out of the death of the Son of God. The cross was not an example for us on how to endure suffering; it was Jesus facing the wrath of God instead of us.

FORSAKEN BY GOD (vv. 1-5)

Jesus did not merely quote these words on the cross; he experienced them. The testimony of God's people down the centuries is to the absolute faithfulness of God. David said in Psalm 37 that he had never seen the righteous forsaken. There was no one more righteous than Jesus but he was forsaken by God. Psalm 22:4 is the normal experience of God's people— they trust in the Lord and he helps them. So why was Christ forsaken by God the Father?

The explanation is to be found in verse 3: God is the Holy One. We have already seen something of the holiness of God and if we ever forget this we shall be in danger of failing to understand the true character of God and why he acts as he does.

The holy God laid our sin and guilt upon his Son and Jesus our substitute bore it alone. On the cross he was facing the wrath and judgment of God upon our sin. That is why the Father turned his back on him. The Bible says that God is so holy that he is of purer eyes than to behold evil and cannot look on iniquity. So when Christ bore our sin he was left to tread the winepress of divine wrath alone. There was no angel to help him, no friend to comfort him, no Holy Spirit to assure him, no smile of a heavenly Father to encourage him. Christ hung on the cross alone with our sins, facing all the hatred of the world and hell, but far worse, facing the holy judgment of the Lord upon the sin of his people.

THE LONELINESS AND AGONY OF THE CROSS (vv. 6-21)

Jesus is the Lord of glory, the express image of God, yet in verse 6 he describes himself as a worm and not even a man. It is sin, our sin, that has done this.

In verses 7 and 8 we see this sin erupt into hatred and scorn of Jesus. Verses 14-17 show us the physical agony of the cross. This is the cost of salvation. This is what sin does. At the cross we see man's hatred of God, but we also see God's hatred of sin as the Holy One deals with the sinner's substitute. Sin is an insult to the holiness of God; it separates man from God and leaves him with no hope in the world.

DELIVERANCE (vv. 22-31)

Calvary is past and now we see something of Christ's triumph. The lament of verse 1 turns into the joyful assurance of verse 24: 'He has not hidden his face from him but has listened to his cry for help.' The forsaking was very real but it was only temporary and now sweet communion is once again enjoyed with the heavenly Father. Sin has been dealt with, divine justice is satisfied and now divine love breaks out in the praise of verse 22 and the worship of verse 29.

And note especially the last glorious proclamation of verses 30 and 31. Future generations will be told—told what? Told what Jesus has done on the cross; told of God's love and grace and mercy and provision of salvation; told of Jesus dying in our place.

THE NEW TESTAMENT JESUS

The Christ of Psalm 22 is the same Christ preached with such power and passion in the New Testament. This can be seen very clearly in the first sermon preached by Peter after the resurrection in Acts 2. Peter does not refer to Psalm 22 but he does quote from Psalm 16 and Psalm 110 as well as from the prophet Joel. His sermon is rooted thoroughly in Old Testament scripture but his message is clearly of a crucified and resurrected Jesus.

There is no life to compare with life in Christ. It is full and complete as we shall see in the next psalm.

Psalm Twenty-Three

A LIFE ENGROSSED IN GOD

Psalm 23 has a special place in the heart of every Christian unrivalled by almost every other portion of Scripture. The depth and beauty of each statement finds either a longing or an echoing response in the believer's heart. The Psalm is one of the most remarkable passages of Scripture because it seems suitable for almost any occasion. Set to music it can be sung with equal suitability at a wedding or a funeral. There is such a breadth to it that it can be applied to most experiences of life. Here we see life in all its fullness.

David's experience of God in this Psalm is one that every true Christian wants. We all desire to know the Lord leading us, guiding us, providing for us and protecting us. We all want to know rest and peace in life and to fear no evil in our dying moments. These are blessings so desirable that we almost instinctively make Psalm 23 a prayer. But David is not praying here. This Psalm is not a prayer for what David wants but a song of thanksgiving for hat he already has.

He is not asking God to do these things for him. He does not say, I hope the Lord will be my Shepherd; he praises God that he already is his Shepherd. David does not theorize about coming to a position at some point in the future when he will lack nothing, but rather delights that because the Lord is his Shepherd he can never lack anything, now or ever. This is the man's experience of God. It is a psalm like this that makes us realize how little we know the Lord. If we are believers we can rejoice in the salvation we have in the Lord Jesus Christ and in that sense we too can say, the Lord is my Shepherd, but do we know the closeness with God that Psalm 23 is obviously describing?

OUR EXPERIENCE

The Psalm is the prayer of many Christians, but it is the experience of very few, so how do we make this our experience? We must certainly get beyond merely admiring the beauty of these words of David. There is no doubt that these are magnificent words that flow with an exquisite beauty, but what about the reality of them? The poetic beauty may do something for some cultural or ascetic need we have, but it does nothing for our soul. An ungodly man can be taken up with the beauty of the Psalm, but our privilege as Christians is to experience the reality of the truths expressed here.

The Bible is not a book of lovely thoughts or fanciful theories, it is a book about God and who he is and what he can do for us. What God was to David he wants to be to all his people. David was not a super saint who knew things of God we can never know. Like us all he was a sinner saved by grace. Just like us he often made a mess of his life, but he knew the reality of God, and if we do not know this reality, we need to start by praying for it.

We have to realize that the close fellowship with God described in this Psalm is possible for us. There is a tendency to denigrate ourselves, and think that the rich blessings so often referred to in Scripture are not for ordinary Christians like us. But there is no such thing as an ordinary Christian. Every Christian is the result of a supernatural activity of God the Holy Spirit. We are all the apple of God's eye and precious and honored in the Lord's sight. It is right to feel unworthy and to be conscious of our sin, but it is wrong to conclude from this that we are doomed to live second rate spiritual lives.

Sadly, many Christians see the failure in their Christian lives and get depressed and think they will never know the joy and blessing that David is delighting in. They know the truth of the first statement that the Lord is my Shepherd, that is they know they have a Savior. They believe in eternal security and the final perseverance of the saints, so they know the truth of the last statement, I will dwell in the house of Lord forever. The problem is that somehow all that is in between in the Psalm seems so remote and unreal, and consequently they know little of the present joy and experience of living for God.

TRUSTING GOD

The despondent believer makes a sad mistake when he allows his sense of unworthiness, which rightly hinders him from trusting in himself, to prevent him from trusting God. The glory of the gospel is that all the way through it takes into account our unworthiness. The gospel was never meant for great people who are capable and worthy but for poor, wretched sinners. Its message is that Christ died for the ungodly and that to such people God offers a free and full salvation. This salvation includes knowing all the blessings of the love of the Heavenly Father here and now in this world.

If we can truly say the Lord is my Shepherd, then we ought to be able to say everything else in Psalm 23. Really the whole Psalm is a commentary on the first statement. If the Lord is my Shepherd, I cannot lack anything, because he is pledged to look after me. Because he is my Shepherd, he makes me lie down in green pastures, he restores my soul, and so on all the way through the Psalm. Our problem is that we get too preoccupied with ourselves and what we are achieving, and not preoccupied enough with the Shepherd and what he has promised to do for us. The message of Psalm 23 to us is, fix your eyes upon the Lord. The whole Psalm is about what God does for us, not what we do for him. David is not one of those believers who is always talking about what he has done for God. Rather he delights in the Lord and trusts him for all his needs.

THE SHEPHERD'S CHOICE

The glory of Psalm 23 is the glory of our privilege as Christians, and we are to rejoice in this. The Lord is the Shepherd, we are the sheep, and the simple fact is that the Shepherd chooses the sheep and not the sheep the Shepherd. Or, to be more accurate, God chooses the sheep and gives them to Jesus the Good Shepherd (John 10:29). There can be no greater privilege than that. It was God who made himself David's Shepherd. Jesse's son did not take upon himself this great privilege, but God called him and brought him into a living relationship with himself.

What God did for David, he has done for all his people. The Lord God in love and mercy has placed himself in relationship to our souls as shepherd to the sheep. There is no rational explanation for this other than that this is a sovereign act of divine love. It is certainly not that we are more worthy of God's love than anyone else. He chooses whom he chooses. There all the argument about the mechanics of this choice must stop, but the implications of it are vast. Not least of these is that it humbles us. This doctrine causes us to see our nothingness, but at the same time there is nothing like it to lift our spirits and reveal to us the wonder of divine grace.

Why is it that so many Christians have trouble with the Shepherd choosing his sheep? Imagine a sheep market with farmers and shepherds milling around intending to increase their flock of sheep. How do they add to their flock? They do not walk past the sheep pens and wait for some animal to bleat its acceptance of them. The sheep do not say I will have the farmer with the green hat to be my shepherd. That would be absurd. It is the farmer who does the choosing. The sheep are passive: they go where they are told.

If we think it is ridiculous for a sheep to choose a man to be its shepherd, how much more ridiculous is it for a miserable creature like sinful man to choose almighty God. It has to be God who chooses. Whatever else may be true or not true of you as a Christian, it is God who has made you one of the sheep of his flock. And he did so knowing everything about you. He knew your weaknesses and failures, but still he chose you. If when we were his enemies God could love us and choose us, he will not love us any less now that we are one of his sheep. This should encourage us to rejoice that nothing can separate us from the love of God.

We are not to take our sin lightly, and it is right that we should mourn over it, but at the same time, even that sin does not cancel the shepherd/sheep relationship. The Bible teaches us to examine our hearts and to recognize our unworthiness, but it never tells us to stop there. If we stop at our sinfulness, we will never know the riches of God's love and grace. See your sin and unworthiness, but then turn the page over and discover a new and glorious chapter. In spite of your sin there is a God, a Shepherd who never stops loving you. All the worth is on God's side. It always was, and always will be.

ABSORBED IN GOD

In Psalm 51 David laments the depth of his sin, but even the he does so against the backcloth of the grace and pardon of loving God. In this he is like all the Bible writers, as the focus of their attention always comes back to the greatness of God. They delight in the love of God, but there they have a problem. How can they find words adequate enough to describe such love? They employ every phrase expressing human affection to try to describe God's love. They use all sorts of illustrations to show us in some measure the greatness 4 God's love. But even the most glorious language and most vivid imagery is inadequate for this task. They do their best and use a great variety of picture language. God is the Rock, the Corner Stone, the Foundation; all to show us something of the immutability of God. Then they change the metaphor: Christ is the Tree of Life, the Root of David, the Righteous Branch, the True Vine. They change the language again and Christ becomes the Light of the World, the Bright an Morning Star, the Sun of Righteousness. Or again, he is the Friend of sinners, our Brother, Father, Husband, Lover of our souls, the Lord our Shepherd. These men, even when inspired by the Holy Spirit to write Scripture, cannot ever come to a final and satisfactory description of God. But God excites them and they are taken up with him. Many of us have problems with prayer. We feel we do not have the words and language others may have, and so we are afraid to pray in public.

We need to realize that the most eloquent language is totally inadequate to do justice to our God. We are all alike as

Christians, just poor sinners in the presence of a loving Father. Words are not the important thing, but w need to be taken up with God, absorbed in God, delight in God.

In Psalm 23 David is clearly lost in the wonder of his God. He may have been thinking of all the blessings God had brought into his life, and he gropes with words to praise the Lord. His language is simple, not profound. His concepts are not vague and mystical, but common and known to all. He simply says, The Lord is my Shepherd. For him this sums up the character of his God. But the point of the Psalm is that he is engrossed in the Lord, and there is no better place for the believer to be.

David glories in the freeness and fullness of divine grace. He rejoices in the exceeding greatness of God's love, that this Almighty God should condescend to be his Shepherd. The language is simple, but the truth is amazing, and the experience of it is breathtaking. In all the circumstances of life God is providing for me, and even when I make a mess of things, God restores my soul. Every day the goodness and mercy of God follow me to minister to my needs. Death itself, that last enemy which has always terrified man, is even subdued by the presence of the Shepherd. How favored David was to know these things, but such blessing is not confined to him alone. All Christians are promised this in salvation. Jesus is the Good Shepherd who died for us, and wants us to have life to the full (John 10:13).

The Psalm is meant to show us the greatness of God and the greatness of our privilege as the people of God. If you are a Christian, you are among the most favored people in the world. You are the most blessed of all people. You may have plenty of problems: David did, but the Lord is your Shepherd, and that outweighs everything else.

Psalm Thirty-Four

A RESTORED LIFE

When a person becomes a Christian he, or she, comes into a living and personal relationship with God. He is now a child of God and a member of the household of faith. The implications of this for that person's life are many and varied. But it does not mean that he never has any more problems or difficulties. Far from it. The experiences of God's people in Scripture show this. David speaks for us all when he wrote, 'A righteous man may have many problems' (Ps. 34:19).

This is so for several reasons. No Christian is sinless and often the repercussions of our sin cause us problems. Sometimes God has to teach us lessons that we will learn only in affliction, and therefore he allows trials to come into our lives. Then, of course, the devil is always seeking to make life difficult for God's people. So problems will come in all shapes and sizes. Therefore the question of most importance is, 'How do we cope with them?'

Psalm 34 is David's reaction to a major problem. The background to his problem is revealed in the introduction to the psalm, 'when he pretended to be insane before Abimelech'. This reference is to the incident in 1 Samuel 21. There is no mention in that chapter of Abimelech, but there is to Ahimelech, so it is easy to assume that they are the same man, but that would be wrong. Abimelech is a title for the Philistine kings, in much the same way as Pharaoh is used for the Egyptian kings. So in 1 Samuel 21 Abimelech is Achish, King of Gath. Ahimelech was a priest who was killed because of David's lies and deceit.

LIES AND DECEIT

David was fleeing for his life from King Saul. When he came to Nob, he told Ahimelech the priest that he was on a secret mission for the king. The priest therefore helped David by giving him bread and Goliath's sword. David then moved on to Gath, a Philistine city, where he was recognized as a dangerous enemy. To escape punishment he pretended to be insane. Achish (Abimelech) therefore let him go free. The whole incident was unsavory and degrading, but it did not end there. The priest, Ahimelech, together with eighty-four other men, was killed on Saul's orders for helping David—and all because of David's lies and deceit.

David must have been at an all-time spiritual low at this point, but even in such an awful spiritual condition he turns to God in this remarkable 34th Psalm. So often as Christians when pressures pile up, when our weaknesses overcome us and we feel hopeless failures, guilt makes us reluctant to pray. We convince ourselves that we must do something to rectify things before we can pray, and thus we deprive ourselves of the blessings of prayer by listening to the lies of Satan.

In our sin, in our failures, whatever the cause, there is only one place for the believer: 'This poor man called, and the Lord heard him; he saved him out of all his troubles' (v. 6). Psalm 34 was written some time after the incident in 1 Samuel 21. It is not the spontaneous cry of a soul in anguish, but David's considered, thought-out reflection as he looks back on the incident. It is a very carefully composed alphabetical psalm, with each of the twenty-two verses beginning with a consecutive letter of the Hebrew alphabet, *Aleph, Beth, Gimel,* etc. For this reason it is more valuable to us. David, coolly and calmly, looks back and wants us to learn from his mistakes. He says in verse 11, 'Come, my children, listen to me; I will teach you the fear of the Lord.'

THIS POOR MAN

What makes a man poor? The first thing that springs to mind would be a lack of money, and this would have been true of David at the time. He was an outlaw, having to beg bread. It is true that his prospects were tremendous—he was chosen by God and the throne was to be his, but at that moment he was poor. All that being so, surely that is not what he meant in verse 6. He was a man after God's own heart, chosen, anointed, with glorious prospects, but in his troubles he did not behave as if these facts were so. He feared man and stooped to lies and deceit. There was no trust in God, and looking back David realizes how wrong he was. Compare Psalm 34:1,13 with the actual events in the presence of Achish. He is ashamed and feels himself to be a poor, miserable failure. This was his poverty.

Do you feel like this? You are a Christian, therefore your prospects are glorious. You love God but you do not always act as if it is so. You feel ashamed, a failure and a poor Christian.

That may all be true; it certainly was of David, but David knew that if he was poor in his own estimation, he was righteous in God's. The same is true of all Christians. Our acceptance by God never depended upon our good deeds, therefore our bad deeds as Christians cannot lose that acceptance for us. Righteousness is a gift of God. It is a grace that comes to us through the gospel, 'For in the gospel a righteousness from God is revealed, a righteousness that is by faith' (Rom. 1:17). We are acceptable to God because of Christ's righteousness, not our own. This does not mean that we can treat sin lightly. Paul argues this out powerfully in Romans 6, and David in Psalm 34 clearly feels his spiritual poverty caused by his own sin. He is broken-hearted and crushed in spirit (v.18), but the Lord is close to such people. They are still God's people, therefore they can cry to the Lord for mercy and forgiveness.

When you feel so poor and begin to think you have no right to pray, remember your right does not depend upon your actions, but upon God's grace. When we are faithless God always remains faithful. He is rich in mercy even when we are poor in faith.

THIS POOR MAN CALLED

Because David was a man of God, certain things were inevitably to be seen in his life. They may have been shrouded by sin for a while but they would emerge again. And this is also true of every believer.

In verse 18 we see his deep conviction of sin; he was broken-hearted and crushed in spirit. For most of us conviction of sin is deeper for sins committed after conversion than anything we ever knew before we were saved. The man who can go on happily in his sin, denying it is wrong and justifying his evil

48

deeds, is no child of God. The Christian is capable of just about any sin, but by the grace of God he will eventually see it for what it is and come back in repentance to the Lord.

Certain other things are also true of the Christian—the poor, guilty, failure of a Christian. He fears God (v. 7), trusts God (v. 8) and seeks God (v.10). It is because these things are true of him that he will call out to God in his hopelessness and desperation. He does not politely petition: he calls, he cries. He is a failure; therefore it is a poor man's cry, depending on nothing in himself. But it is a powerful cry and is always effective because the Lord both hears and answers it.

THE GOODNESS OF GOD

In the psalm our gaze is taken from the poor man to the infinite goodness of God. David reminds us that the Lord is attentive (v. 15); the Lord hears (v. 17); the Lord delivers (v. 17); the Lord is close (v. 18); the Lord saves (v. 18); the Lord delivers (v. 19); the Lord redeems (v. 22). What a God! He is worthy of our trust, our praise and our adoration. This is why David begins the psalm with three verses of delighting in the Lord.

It was not David's lies and deceit that got him out of his troubles, but the Lord. We have no need as Christians to resort to guile and deceit to avoid trouble. God is always to be our refuge and strength. The world's ways are not for God's people. They always dishonor God and make us spiritually poor.

Does God always hear and save us out of our troubles? He always hears but sometimes he tells us, as he did Paul in 2

Corinthians 12:7-10, 'I will not take your problem away but I will give you grace to cope with it.'

The consequence of such an answer for Paul was: 'I delight in weaknesses, in insults, in hardships, in persecutions, in difficulties. For when I am weak, then I am strong.'

Our problems may be as a result of our own sin, like David's in Psalm 34. They may be like Paul's, as part of God's dealing with us in grace. They may be a direct attack of the devil. Whichever is true, there is only one thing for the Christian to do—cry to God and look for his intervention.

Psalm Forty-Nine

A LIFE THAT TRANSCENDS DEATH

Here is a psalm addressed to 'all who live in the world'. The writer is casting his net wide. He believes he has something to say to every living man and woman. He is convinced that his words are applicable to all and are always relevant and this is so because his subject is the twin realities of life and death. He considers how temporary life is. No one can live forever—the wise and the foolish both come to the same end (v. 10). All that a man may achieve in this life has to be left behind and 'their tombs will remain their houses forever' (v. 11). Verse 14 is a devastating commentary on human life, 'Like sheep they are destined for the grave.'

No one can disagree with the truth of this and if this is all that man has to look forward to then life would indeed be pointless. We all like to think that there must be more to it than this. The psalmist says, yes there is, and points us to the God who can redeem our life from the grave (v. 15).

MEN AND BEASTS

The great pursuit of man is for riches and power, and this is because they are supposed to be able to bring him happiness and security. The psalmist admits there is an element of truth in this, but only an element. Wealth and posterity will bring the praise of men (v. 18). But the fallacy of this pursuit is that it ignores the inevitability of death. Riches do not bring security because all men are 'like the beasts that perish' (v. 12).

Such a statement does not do our ego much good and will arouse a violent disagreement from us. Are not human beings obviously superior to the beasts? Did not even God recognize this in Genesis 2:19 when he allowed man to name the beasts? This is true, but in terms of death man is like the beasts. He must and will die. But that is not all there is to it. For man the grave is not the end. Death does not have the last word.

Man has an immortal soul. He is not an animal but a being made in the image of God, therefore for man there is something beyond the grave—'But God will redeem my life from the grave; he will surely take me to himself' (v. 15). This is the great truth that finds its glorious fulfillment in the Lord Jesus Christ. But it is not guaranteed for everyone. In fact, verses 7-9 seem to rule it out for all of us. 'No man can redeem the life of another or give to God a ransom for him—the ransom for a life is costly, no payment is ever enough—that he should live on forever and not see decay'.

If the redemption and ransom had to be provided by us it would be an impossibility, but it is God who redeems and pays the ransom. In the Bible redemption and ransom have no significant meaning unless they are interpreted in the context of human sin and divine wrath. This is always the case in the New Testament. We are redeemed from all wickedness (Titus 2:4); the grip of sin (Romans 6); the old life (1 Peter 1:18); the curse of the law (Galatians 3:13); and the bondage of the law (Galatians 4:5).

MAN IN SIN

All mankind is in captivity to sin. We are slaves to our own corrupt and depraved nature. This is a bondage of the mind, the will and the spirit that is so powerful that if left to ourselves freedom is impossible. That is what Psalm 49 is saying. It is not decrying wealth and wisdom as useless, it is merely saying that without God they have no worth and no eternal value. Though they may make life more pleasant they are impotent in the face of death.

Sin may be defined as man, whether rich or poor, wise or foolish, living with no regard for God. That puts him inevitably into bondage to sin. From this he must be set free, or his immortal soul will go to hell. The problem is that he cannot free himself, he cannot redeem himself and no one else can do it for him. The reason is spelt out in verses 7-8, the cost is too great.

Sin is rebellion against God. It is an affront to the holiness and character of God. Our problem is that we do not see sin like that. We trivialize it and make it of no account. But God will not have that. Man is a sinner and that sin has to be dealt with.

If man was spiritually free there would be no need of redemption; but our slavery to sin is real. It is not an illusion but the common fact about every human being. Sin is a great deceiver. It holds before us endless pleasures but fails to tell of the price or consequence of following its attractions. In Genesis 3 the awful reality of sin is shown to us. Then in the next chapter we see the effects of sin as a man kills his own brother. By the time we get to Genesis 6 sin's dominance is seen in every human being as 'every inclination of the thoughts of his heart was only evil all the time' (v. 5).

In the New Testament the power of sin comes to its terrible climax when men kill the Son of God. From then on, the New Testament spells out sin's consequences in frightening clarity in passages like Romans 1:18-32. In Romans 7 Paul puts into words the experience of every man and woman: 'We know that the law is spiritual; but I am unspiritual, sold as a slave to sin. I do not understand what I do. For what I want to do I do not do, but what I hate I do' (vv. 14-15).

It is from this bondage that Jesus came to redeem us.

Redemption means to buy out of slavery, but the purchase price to set us free from sin is enormous. The price is infinitely beyond anything we could afford. This is why Peter says that we are not redeemed with silver or gold but with the precious blood of the Lamb of God (1 Peter 1:18-19). Only Jesus could pay that price.

RANSOM

Jesus told us that the reason he came into the world was 'to give his life as a ransom for many' (Mark 10:45). The word ransom is familiar to us when we read of someone who has been kidnapped and a ransom price is demanded to set him free. Jesus teaches us that his death is the means by which we are set free. He gave his life as the price of freedom for the slaves of sin. Redemption is a costly business. Peter has reminded us of that, and so too does Paul: 'In him we have redemption through his blood, the forgiveness of sins, in accordance with the riches of God's grace' (Ephesians 1:7).

The ransom price is the blood of Jesus, or, in other words, his sacrificial death on the cross. We are not redeemed by the teaching of Jesus or by the fact that he could do miracles. It is what he did on the cross that purchased our salvation.

54

We are not to think that the ransom price was paid to Satan as if he had some right to the payment. It is true we were the slaves of sin, but Satan's power was that of an invader or usurper. He had no rights of ownership. It was God who made us and all the rights are his. So the ransom price was paid to satisfy the demands of God's law which we had violated by our sin. The law demanded that the wages of sin be the death of the sinner. Christ satisfied that demand on behalf of his people when he shed his blood on the cross. He took full responsibility for our sin. This included its guilt and punishment, and his death is the only payment that is acceptable to God.

Redemption is all of God and that is why the psalmist is so confident in verse 15—'God will redeem my life.' The life the Christian has transcends death and will take him eventually to be with God for all eternity. Has this truth ever struck you in a personal way? How will you respond to him?

Psalm Fifty-One

A LIFE OF REPENTANCE

There can be no salvation without repentance and there can be no repentance without conviction of sin.

Repentance has two sides; it is a turning from sin and God (Acts 3:19). For true repentance both these elements are essential. A man can turn from sin without turning to God. He may see the value of changing his lifestyle and decide to refrain from certain bad habits. No doubt this will do him good in many ways, but spiritually it will be *useless*. On the other hand, a man may turn to God and cry for mercy, but have no intention of leaving his sin. His eyes may be wet with tears and his heart as hard as stone.

True repentance involves seeing sin for what it really is; not just a character defect, but also a permanent attitude of rebellion against the love and care and righteous authority of God. It is this new understanding of God and of one's own sin that leads to true repentance. There will also be a great desire to break with the past and to live in the future only to please God (Acts 26:20). That is repentance.

Repentance does not stop when we are saved. After regeneration we are still sinners and sadly we still break the law of God. The Christian life is a continual battle with sin therefore repentance has to be a daily experience. In fact it is often the case that the believer knows a deeper conviction of sin and a deeper sense of repentance after conversion than he did before. David's prayer of repentance in Psalm 51 is an example of this.

We are to repent every day for the sin of that day. Sin that is not confessed and repented of will fester in our hearts and destroy our fellowship with God.

WHAT IS CONVICTION OF SIN?

It is not 'conviction of sin' for a man to feel bad because he is drinking too much or generally making a mess of his life. Sin is not just a violation of social standards. To see sin only in social or moral terms will not lead people to conviction. Sin must be seen in the light of the law and holiness of God. The gospel is not an aspirin for the aches of life, to soothe and comfort man in misery. It is a holy God's answer to the violation of divine law by human beings whose very nature is to rebel against him.

A sinner can hear the gospel and not make head or tail of it unless he is convinced of sin, unless he first sees his own helplessness and hopelessness. He must see that he is not meeting God's demands and that he can never meet them. He must see his sin in relationship to God and the function of the law is to show him just that. The law makes no attempt to compare one man with another; it takes us all to the yardstick of the holiness of God and there we all fail miserably.

We have seen that repentance does not finish at conversion; it is an on-going fact in our lives because we still sin even as believers. Psalm 51 is the prayer of repentance of a man who had lived very close to God. But even such men sin. The sin David repents of is recorded for us in 2 Samuel 11:1-27.

The sin of David with Bathsheba, and the murder of her husband Uriah to which it led, is one of the saddest stories in the Old Testament. This sin was not committed by some ungodly man who cared nothing for the Lord, but by a deeply spiritual man whom God himself described as 'a man after my own heart'. David had known heights of spiritual blessing and experience that most Christians can only dream about. He had written some of the most glorious and beautiful spiritual songs ever composed. Yet this man sinned in a most terrible way.

We acknowledge that no Christian is perfect and that all believers sin, but this sin of David's was no sudden flash of temper or moment of selfishness. It was deliberate adultery and scheming murder. We are not to stand in judgment with a superior 'holier-than-thou' attitude, but neither are we casually to accept sin as if it were just a moral hiccup. David was no inexperienced youngster, but a man of about fifty. Here is the sin of a good man and we have to learn from it.

HARD IN SIN

David was now married to Bathsheba and the son born of his sin was rocking in a cradle in the palace. Every moment of every day there was this visible reminder to the king of what he had done. But there was no repentance. Everyone knew of the great evil David had done, but he was the king and could get away with it. It seemed that even God was not too concerned because heaven was silent on the matter. For a year there was no repentance and God left David in this condition.

Here we see a very spiritual man deep in the grip of his own sin and refusing to repent. It is not an unusual scene because we can all be like this. Our sin may not be as vile as David's, but the question is not one of the degree of sin, but how we deal with it. It appears that David was not prepared to deal with it. A year had gone by and in all probability another year would have come and gone without any response from the king.

How did David feel? What was he thinking? Did he think no one cared? God had said nothing, so perhaps God did not care either. David knew God well enough to know that this was not true. But as Christians we easily delude ourselves when guilty of sin and as time goes on the delusion gets stronger.

The baby had already been born, so it must have been about a year after the sin was committed that God sent Nathan to David. If David was tempted to think that God had overlooked his sin he was in for a rude awakening.

Nathan was a wise man. He did not go straight up to the king and read the riot act. There are times when that approach is necessary, but not here. David had lived with his sin for a year and could easily have reacted with violent indignation if confronted directly. So Nathan told him a story.

There were two men, one very rich and the other poor. The rich man had many sheep, but the poor man had only one pet lamb. A visitor came to the rich man and, rather than kill one of his many sheep to feed the guest, he stole the poor man's pet lamb and killed it for the meal.

David had no intimation of what Nathan was doing. There had been no repentance, even if he had been under conviction of sin, so he was still blind to the terrible nature of his actions. He was

like the man in the Sermon on the Mount who could clearly see
the speck of sawdust in someone else's eye but could not see the
plank in his own. So he was passionately angry against the rich
man in Nathan's story and demanded that he be put to death.
Isn't it strange that most of us are totally intolerant of the very
sin in others of which we ourselves are guilty?

From his own mouth David had convicted himself and Nathan
simply, but devastatingly, announced, 'You are the man!' This
brought from the king the confession: 'I have sinned against the
Loud.' At last he had come to repentance and the depth of this
can be seen in Psalm 51. Repentance is always followed by
forgiveness: 'The Lord has taken away your sin' (2 Samuel 12:13).
Repentance is not an easy way out because even though there is
forgiveness there are still consequences of sin which have to be
borne: 'But because by doing this you have made the enemies of
the Lord show utter contempt, the son born to you will die' (2
Samuel 12:14).

Repentance leads to forgiveness; this does not bypass the
consequences of sin, but it does lead to restoration to the Lord:
'He went into the house of the Lord and worshipped' (2 Samuel
12:20).

REPENTANCE

It would be impossible to understand Psalm 51 without seeing its
historical background. Our background is probably very different
but all sin needs to be repented of.

In verses 3-6 he makes his confession of sin and he gives no
excuses; it is my transgression, my sin. Sin is our personal
responsibility, and even though (as v 5 correctly teaches us) we
are sinners by nature, each separate act of sin is our own

deliberate rebellion against the law of God. David had very clearly sinned against Uriah, but here he acknowledges that all sin is against God (v 4). This is a very solemn thought. The poison of sin lies in its opposition to almighty God, and when we sin against each other, we are sinning against God.

So David confesses his personal guilt (v 3), his corrupt nature (v 5) and his rebellion against God (v 4).

Confession is an indispensable condition of pardon but God forgives not merely because we confess. David's hope for pardon rests in the mercy, unfailing love and great compassion of the Lord (vv. 1-2).

Sin pollutes and leaves an ugly stain, so the sinner must be washed and cleansed, and the sin blotted out. Hyssop (v 7) was a little shrub with which the blood and water of purification were applied under the law of God. So David is asking God to cleanse him by the means he has provided. God's appointed means to deal with our sin is the blood of the Lord Jesus Christ.

Remember that Psalm 51 is the prayer of a child of God. In other words, here is the repentance of a converted man. Repentance is necessary throughout the Christian's life when he is aware of sin in his heart.

Nathan very strongly reminded David that there are no secret sins before God. It is utter foolishness to think that we can deceive God by our so-called 'secret sins'. We should always fear sin because it grieves the heart of God and robs us of the joy of our salvation. Sin will never do us any good. It may for a while give great pleasure; it may get you a better job and more money; it may help you avoid some troubles; but eventually it will rob you, impoverish you and make you as miserable as it is itself.

In many ways what was worse than David's sin was his refusal to repent. We all sin. That is not an excuse, but it is a fact. When God awakens your conscience flee to him in confession and repentance. Don't let Satan keep you in sin, and don't let the Evil One deceive you into thinking that your sin means you are finished for ever as a Christian. There is always forgiveness when there is repentance.

Psalm Fifty-Nine

A DIFFICULT LIFE

God never promised his people an easy life. Even a casual reading of the lives of the men and women in the Bible will show this. Difficulties are never far away. Sometimes they come as a result of our own foolishness and sin, but sometimes we can genuinely feel that we did nothing to earn that particular difficulty.

Often our problems are ones of redemption. Take for instance the Israelites in Exodus 14. If they had not been redeemed they would not have faced these particular problems. The difficulties were the Red Sea in front of them and the Egyptians behind them. They were no phantom problems but very real and serious - so much so that the Israelites were terrified and saw no way out of their predicament.

These people had recently been redeemed. All their lives they had been in slavery with no hope of rescue. But God had loved them and chosen them and exerted divine power to set them free. They had sheltered under the blood of the Passover lamb and had been led in triumph from their bondage. God had done it and they knew it was the only way they could have obtained redemption. Slavery was behind them and they were on their way to the Promised Land.

What was true of them is also true of all Christians. We are redeemed from the bondage of sin. Our situation was hopeless but God loved us and chose us and, by exerting the divine power of grace, love and mercy, he saved us. The bondage of sin is behind us and heaven is before us. Of all people in this world none is as favored and privileged as the Christian.

It was because of the blessing of redemption that the Israelites' difficulties arose. If they had not been redeemed they would never have been in the particular situation that terrified them. We need to appreciate that there are trials peculiar to the Christian and these are the direct result of coming out of the world. Far from being exempt from problems - as is sometimes suggested by the 'Come to Jesus and be happy' type of preaching - the Christian has to face all the difficulties that confront the non Christian, such as health worries, family problems and financial concerns, plus a host of spiritual problems of which the unbeliever knows nothing. These are problems of redemption, of new life in Christ. They are part of the spiritual battle and Satan's opposition.

PROBLEMS

David was in a similar situation when he wrote Psalm 59—'See how they lie in wait for me! Fierce men conspire against me for no offence or sin of mine, O Lord. I have done no wrong, yet they are ready to attack me.' (v.3-4). The introduction to the Psalm tells us it arose from the time when Saul sent men to watch David's house in order to kill him. The story is recorded in 1 Samuel 18 & 19.

David would readily admit that he was a sinner, but on this particular occasion he knew he had done nothing to deserve the pressure that threatened to crush him. It is true that there are times when the chastening of the Lord comes upon us because of some sin, but it is wrong to say that every difficult period or problem in our lives is the result of a particular sin. Job's comforters made that mistake and some Christians still do. David was in trouble, but 'for no offence or sin of mine' (v.3).

Do you know this experience? Pressures build up in your life until you feel almost overwhelmed. It comes to us all, sometimes in our family life, or in church affairs or at work. What we can learn from Psalm 59 is how to face such situations and triumph over them. If we can learn David's reaction to these problems we will learn lessons to benefit us right through life. Indeed it may help us to understand why God allows these clouds to come over us.

PRAYER

David commences the Psalm by casting himself upon God for deliverance. He prays himself out of a sense of helplessness into quiet confidence, and he concludes with a burst of victorious song. The situation does not change, the enemies are still there but David is at peace in the presence of his loving God. Traps and snares are laid for him at every turn, but he escapes panic and finds rest in the Lord.

The answer to problems is prayer, but prayer will only be of help if we have a true understanding of the God we are praying to. In verse 5 David addresses God as the 'Lord God Almighty, the God of Israel.' He seems to accumulate all the titles he can think of to call heaven to his aid. It is not prayer that changes things but the God to whom pray. Our view of

God will govern the confidence with which we pray. David's confidence is huge as he delights in the God who laughs at his enemy's activities (v.8). Such a God can be our strength and fortress (v.17) in times of trouble.

What was true of David is true of all believers in similar circumstances. If you are in a position in life that God has placed you in you know that you can lay hold on all his power to see you through. Your surrender to God in Christ means that he has guaranteed to be with you in all your problems. If God can make the whole of creation he can care for you in all your needs.

LOOK UP

In the first seven verses David describes his enemies, but then in verses 8-9 his focus changes. He looks up and sees the glory and majesty of his God. Within the compass of these verses David has prayed himself out of any panic or despair he might have had and into a joyful confidence. The circumstances have not changed, but now instead of focusing on the problems, David says, 'I watch for you' (v.9).

It is no use having the Lord as our strength and fortress unless we look to him and watch and wait for him to come to our aid. If we fail to receive strength it is usually because we are not looking for it. We pray but do not wait. We ask but do not expect to receive. We knock but go away before the door is opened to us. It may be that our hands are so full of other things and our eyes looking in the wrong direction that we can never receive the mercies of God.

Psalm 130:6 says, 'My soul waits for the Lord, more than watchmen wait for the morning.' Have you ever waited for the morning? Perhaps you had a restless night of tossing and turning. You could not sleep and long for the morning to come. That is the idea here in the words of the psalmist.

Do not believe the saying, which declares that God helps those who help themselves. God helps those who look to him and depend upon him. This divine help comes to those who are not indifferent, but watch expectantly. It comes to Christians who in the thick of the fight depend upon the Lord. It comes to the one who believes he can do all things through Christ who strengthens him. It comes to the believer who knows that before he calls God will answer. It is faith that turns distress into singing.

From Psalm 59 we need to learn that under the clouds of life when things look impossible, even then we are held in the firm grip of a loving, caring heavenly Father.

Psalm Sixty-Two

A LIFE IN STRESS

Prolonged illness or bereavement inevitably brings pressures upon the Christian. In this area of life the Christian is no different from the non-Christian. The difference will be in how the Christian copes with the stress of illness and death.

In Psalm 62 we find David under great stress. What has caused it we do not know. Some think this psalm was written at the time of his son Absalom's rebellion against him. David was put off the throne by his son and we can imagine the stress that would cause him. Whether this is the background to the psalm or not does not matter; what is important is how David coped with the stress.

In verses 3 and 4 David describes something of the problem he is facing. This is causing him very real difficulties, but there is no depression or fear. Here is great encouragement for us. Stress and fear do not have to go together. Sadly, so often one leads to the other, but there is no necessity for this if you are a Christian. How can we avoid fear and depression while under stress?

SPEAKING TO OURSELVES

We need to learn to speak to ourselves about God, to tell our souls to find rest in God alone. It is said that when a man talks to himself it is the first sign of madness. I do not know how true that is, but I do know that when a Christian can talk to himself about God it is a sure sign of spiritual health. In verse 5 David tells his soul to find rest in God alone. He reminds himself that God is his rock and salvation and his fortress, and because this is true, then in spite of the pressures, he will not be shaken. He is reminding himself who God is and what God has done for him.

This is important, because all too often stress tends to produce an introverted self-pity which sees no hope. There are very few things more damaging for a Christian than self-pity. The remedy for this is to see God in all his glory, which will produce in us a most reasonable optimism. No believer can wallow in self-pity when he is aware that his hope comes from God. The magnificence and benevolence of God are our hope and strength, and when we dwell on these truths, even though the problems do not go away we begin to see them in perspective. If you just dwell on the problem and forget God, then you will see no answer, no hope, and you are left with depression.

The Christian does not believe in bypassing problems. We do not whistle in the dark and pretend the difficulties are not there. That is foolishness. That is what tranquillizers and alcohol do. They make you feel at peace, but the problem has not been faced or dealt with. Whatever is causing us difficulties, whether it is illness, death or anything else, these things are real and have to be faced. But face them in the context of the greatness of the God who loves you. This we do by learning to talk to ourselves about God.

Surely this is part of what the Bible calls meditation. It is to be still and remind ourselves of God. The hymn-book is a wonderful help in this. Just turn over the pages and read the hymns and you will be reminded of the greatness of God. A good hymn-book is one that is full of the goodness and magnificence of God. The great hymns always show you God, and your heart is warmed and encouraged. This helps you and then you will be able to help others in need. In Psalm 62 David spends seven verses delighting in God; only then in verse 8 does he encourage others to do the same.

This is something very practical. Have you ever tried to encourage some other Christian who is going through a rough time? Your motive is right and you say all the right things but you know as you speak that you are not helping him. Why not? Is it not because all you are giving him is words, and he needs more than words? To really be a help we need to come to such people from the presence of God, with our minds and hearts, as well as our words, full of the greatness of God. Talk to yourself first about God; then when you talk to others something of the very fragrance of God will be conveyed to them.

KNOWING OURSELVES

David was a great man, with many God-given gifts, but under pressure he saw himself as a 'leaning wall' and a 'tottering fence'. What a vivid description this is! Have you ever seen a leaning wall? The foundations are insecure, frost has got into the cement and the whole thing is in a state of collapse. One little push and it would be over. The tottering fence is the same. The wooden posts in the ground have rotted. Neglect and wear have taken their toll and it looks as if a strong wind would bring it down. That is how David saw himself in his problems—no stability, no permanence, no strength, nothing to admire, all so frail and on the verge of collapse. He was beginning to see that all that men put their trust in, position and wealth (vv. 9-10), count for nothing in the end.

Such a view would drive most men to despair. But not the Christian, because his rest and hope and strength are not found in himself, but in God alone.

THEORY OR REALITY

No true Christian would dispute this. We find this is the teaching of Scripture and we accept it, but is it just theory to us, or is it a reality? The answer to this will depend on whether or not our priorities are correct. Jesus asked, 'What good will it be for a man if he gains the whole world, yet forfeits his soul?' The soul of man must be our first priority and David, in spite of the precarious position in which he found himself, was able to be at peace because his soul had found rest in God.

What is the soul? It is not an easy word to define and Christians disagree over its precise meaning, but for our purposes I will define the soul as that which distinguishes man from all other created beings, and it is immortal. When God breathed into Adam he became a living soul. It is our souls that give us our worth; therefore when Jesus said, 'Do not be afraid of those who kill the body but cannot kill the soul. Rather, be afraid of the One who can destroy both soul and body in hell,' he was emphasizing the supreme value and priority of the soul. Jesus never taught that the body was unimportant. On the contrary, he cared for people's bodies, he healed them and fed them, but the soul takes top priority.

We need to learn this, and sometimes it is only acute stress that reveals whether or not we really do believe it. Let me give you an example. In August 1985 I was preaching at an open-air service on the promenade in Aberystwyth, Wales. I stressed to the listening crowd the importance and consequence of knowing God. I said the Christian was sure to go to heaven because of the salvation he had in Christ. I said if I was to die tonight I knew I would go to heaven. I believed this and preached it passionately, but ten minutes after preaching I had a heart attack and finished up in hospital. As I lay there all the words that I had been preaching with such passion and enthusiasm began to challenge me. Did I really believe them? The heart attack had suddenly brought the whole issue of life and death into clearer focus. I was now faced with the reality of all that I thought I believed. How do we Christians cope in such situations?

David said, 'My soul finds rest in God alone.' Rest in God, not only in the good times but also in the bad. When the body is racked with pain, when the emotions are bruised and torn in bereavement—even then we can find rest.

FINDING REST

Soul rest is not something that comes automatically, because sadly some do not experience it in times of stress. It is a rest that has to be found. You find something in one of two ways: either accidentally or by searching. Often you do not even know that something exists, so consequently you do not look for it, but suddenly, accidentally, you find it. On the other hand, you are aware of something that you do not possess, so you search for it. There can be a lot of frustration and disappointment in searching, but if you are desperate enough you do not give up until you find. Rest of soul is not found accidentally, but by searching. You know it is possible because God has promised it. You know as a Christian you ought to have it and need it, so you search. In other words you look to God. You ask. You pray and you do not give up until you find it. We shall see in the next chapter from Psalm 63 how to find this rest, but for the moment let us ask, 'What is rest of soul?'

REST OF SOUL

In Psalm 62 David is in trouble and he realizes how weak he is—nothing but a leaning wall and a tottering fence. But he does not stop there. He looks beyond his difficulties to the greatness and goodness of God. Rest of soul is to get things into perspective. It is to realize what we are and what we have in God. We have salvation (v. 1). We have strength because God is our rock (v. 2). We have security because God is our fortress (v. 2). We have stability because we shall never be moved or shaken (v. 2). We have hope (v. 5) and honor (v. 7). All these blessings are to be found in God alone. They can be found nowhere else. They are mercies that do not merely come from God; they are only found in God. You cannot have them in detachment from God. God is not like a doctor who gives you a prescription and you go away and benefit from the remedy. Rest of soul is found in God, in oneness and fellowship with God. It is dependent upon the union we have with Christ.

This rest is not an emotional feeling. It is certainly not gritting your teeth and bearing it stoically. It is not putting on a brave face in time of trouble. Rest of soul is resting in and embracing and experiencing the beauty and wonder of our God and Savior. It is enjoying God when you may not be enjoying much else. It is not something theoretical, but a deep reality of the peace and love and sufficiency of God. It is rest in him.

Psalm Sixty-Three

A LIFE THAT FINDS REST

In the previous chapter we saw from Psalm 62 that the Christian under great stress can know rest of soul, but this does not come automatically. It has to be found. In Psalm 63 David tells us how to find it. In the midst of problems and pressures we are not to sit around and mope with a vague hope that things will get better: we are to seek earnestly.

It is easier to say this than to do it, and while all believers in times of comfort will acknowledge that this is the correct thing to do, when the stress comes we seem to get confused and uncertain. David was aware of this and he realized that we need an incentive to seek God. This man of God is not theorizing but facing real problems. Charles Spurgeon wrote, 'This was probably written while David was fleeing from Absalom; certainly at the time he wrote it he was king (v. 11), and hard pressed by those who sought his life. David did not leave off singing because he was in the wilderness, neither did he in slovenly idleness go on repeating Psalms intended for other occasions; but he carefully made his worship suitable to his circumstances, and presented to his God a wilderness hymn when he was in the wilderness. There was no desert in his heart, though there was a desert around him. We too may expect to be cast into rough places ere we go hence. In such seasons, may the Eternal Comforter abide with us, and cause us to bless the Lord at all times, making even the solitary places to become a temple for Jehovah.'

If we are to know the Eternal Comforter with us then we need to listen to David's advice. The incentive he had to seek God is expressed in Psalm 63:2,3: 'I have seen you in the sanctuary and beheld your power and glory,' and because of this the psalmist could say, 'Your love is better than life.'

OUR INCENTIVE TO SEEK GOD

The incentive to seek God is that we are clear in our minds as to who God is and what he is to his people. In other words, the incentive to seek is that you know there is someone and something to be found. If a man goes prospecting for gold it is because, rightly or wrongly, he believes there is gold to be found. His believing prompts his seeking.

We may come into situations, caused by illness, bereavement or something else, and begin to think there is no answer. But because we are Christians we know there is an answer. We may not have it at the moment, but we know it is to be found. The answer is God and, whatever problem we have to face, we can always say like David, 'O God, you are my God.' Nothing changes that. If this is true, why is it that we have to seek God? The answer is because the problems so often overwhelm us and we lose sight of God. He is still there, but we allow the problems to block him out. Our doctrine may still be perfectly all right but our experience of God has gone haywire. We succumb to the pressures and our view of God is lost, or at best confused.

In such situations we should do as David did. We must draw on past experiences. That is what verse 2 is about. There was no sanctuary in the desert of Judah, but that did not prevent David from remembering past blessings and experiences of God. I am not encouraging us to live in the past. You cannot live on past blessings, but you can use them as an incentive to seek God and know those blessings again. This is what David is doing. When there is darkness in the soul and you can find no help from Scripture or worship or fellowship, and those things that were once a blessing to you, you now avoid, —we can all know periods like this—then your only hope is to remember better days and richer experiences of God. Remember the times when prayer was a joy and fellowship a delight, when the Word spoke so clearly and so often to you. Your hope is that God is unchanging and what you knew once you can know again.

HOW TO SEEK GOD

We are to seek earnestly, and there are two reasons for this. The first is the character of God, and the second is the desperate need we have. The picture painted in this psalm is very vivid. When a man is lost in a desert there is only one thing he wants. You can offer him wealth, fame, position or promotion, but he is not interested. These things are of no more value to him than the sand under his feet. The only thing he wants is water. His whole life is reduced to one basic requirement—water.

Similarly, a Christian under stress, that has perhaps led him into a spiritual desert, says with David,

> 'My soul thirsts for you, my body longs for you,
> in a dry and weary land where there is no water.'

79

That is earnest seeking. This man is not playing at Christianity. Every atom and fiber of his being long for God. Nothing else will satisfy him. He will not be satisfied with a little blessing from God; he wants God himself. This man is now taken up with God more than his problems. In verse 6 he tells us that he cannot get God out of his mind. He cannot sleep because he is thinking about God. Our problem so often is that we cannot sleep because we are worrying about our difficulties. Remember David is not writing this during a period of ease and comfort, but in a time of acute difficulties, and his problems have not gone away. He tells us in verses 9 and 10 that his enemies are still active, but he is not worried about them because he knows he is in God's hands and God will deal with them.

At this point rest of soul is beginning to make itself known to David. Peace is drawing near. The problem is still real, but God is more real. Rest of soul is not some magical experience; it is simply seeking God before all things. When God is in the centre of the Christian's focus, even though the problems still have to be dealt with, then there is rest and peace. This is not some glib, easy remedy; it is getting to grips with God. In Psalm 62:8 David describes it as pouring out your heart to him. This will involve not only bringing our fears and sorrows to God, but also our sin and disobedience. Very often the greatest stress caused to the Christian is an unwillingness to go God's way. On many occasions our difficulties are caused not originally by our *actions*, but by our *reactions* to people and situations. We may be suffering unjustly, but the way we cope with that may be sinful. 'Pour out your heart to God', says David, 'and trust him at all times.' Then, and only then, will we stay close to God and know that the divine hand upholds (Ps. 63:8).

The Christian finds rest of soul when he is acutely aware of his own weakness and of the infinite greatness and goodness of

God. In God alone is rest, and the result in Psalm 63 is praise (v. 4), satisfaction (v. 5), joy (v. 11) and a determination (v. 8) to stay close to God and not lose again the sense of the presence and peace of God. Our hope is the character of God, and in times of great difficulties our hope for deliverance is not in the pastor, or the church, or Christian friends (though we thank God for these), but our hope is in God alone. So we are to seek him earnestly, and we do so in the knowledge that he is already seeking us. 'Seek and you will find.'

Psalm Sixty-Six

A JOYFUL LIFE

The man who wrote this psalm is obviously excited and thrilled by his God. He clearly is full of the joy of the Lord. Not for him the cold, formal, nominal religion that seems to satisfy so many. Not for him empty religious jargon and cold platitudes. God is alive to him. God is real and he delights in his God.

The whole psalm is full of passion, reality and vigor. But it is not the passion of charged emotionalism, or the vigor of a worked up and controlled service. In verses 1-4 it is as if he can hardly contain himself in wanting to praise and adore the Lord. Why is this? It is obviously the result of his experience of God. Just to know facts about God will never produce the exhilaration of these verses. Do we know anything of this? Take for example v. 3, 'How awesome are your deeds'. Do you ever say that to God? Do we see the awesomeness of God's deeds in our lives?

Here is a man whose eyes are open. So many believers lose the joy and thrill of their faith because their eyes are shut. They don't see and appreciate what the Lord is doing. Coupled with this they have short memories of blessings received and forget how good God has been to them. See the psalmist in verse 4, he seems to see every tree and blade of grass praising the Lord. That is not foolish romanticism but a redeemed soul with his eyes open and drinking in the mercies of God.

Then in verse 5, he addresses all of us. He calls us to consider the works of God on our behalf.

GOD'S REDEEMING WORK   verses 6-7

The reference is to the Red Sea and the passage out of slavery into the Promised Land. In other words he reminds the people of their redemption. Have you ever noticed how many times in the Old Testament reference is made back to the Passover and the Red Sea? It does so because this is the greatest thing that ever happened to them. If you question that, you ought to seriously consider if you know anything of true biblical salvation.

Charles Wesley was converted on May 21, 1738 and exactly one year later he wrote a hymn that used to be prefixed in the Methodist hymnbook as a hymn to commemorate ones conversion. The hymn was, 'O for a thousand tongues to sing my great redeemers praise". The psalmist would have said, Amen, to that.

God's work of redemption is always sovereign—'he rules forever by his power' (v. 7). God works not by permission, nor assistance, not even with the co-operation of men, but always by his power. And are we not glad that it is so? Would not the Israelites have been glad of this? Pharaoh said no to their redemption, and they themselves were not all that keen. But God did it. Thank God that he did not leave the decision to Pharaoh or to them. They did everything but co-operate, but

God saved them. The same is true of our salvation. It was not that we decided to be saved. God saved us.

Are we not glad that salvation is of the Lord. Many people and influences would have held us back. Many of us did everything but co-operate, but God saved us. How awesome are God's works. When we consider our salvation we will inevitably have to praise the Lord.

GOD'S PRESERVING WORK   verses 8-9

I sometimes think that God's preserving work is more amazing than his redeeming work. That God saved me as a teenager was amazing, but that 50 years later I am still a Christian is staggering.

In spite of all my waywardness since he has kept my feet from slipping (v. 9). When you think of all the sin in your life since you were saved; some sin you slipped into unintentionally, but others you walked into deliberately; yet God has not written you off. He still loves you and has not disowned you. And it is not because he does not mind our sin. It deeply grieves and hurts him, but still he keeps on and preserves us.

That is amazing grace. We are saved by grace and kept by grace. No wonder the psalmist encourages us in verse 8 to praise the Lord, and he adds, do it with enthusiasm so that it can be heard.

Many years ago I was in a prayer meeting and a man was praying and delighting in God. He came to a part in his prayer when he wanted to thank God for preserving him, but he could not think of the word. His mind had gone blank. But that did not stop him and he blurted out "thank you Lord for pickling me". We all laughed because it sounded so funny but it was a perfectly appropriate word. The dictionary defines pickled as to be immersed in vinegar or a similar liquid to preserve. All believers are preserved in the grace of God and this preserves for eternity.

GOD'S REFINING WORK verses 10-12

This work of God is not very pleasant or comfortable to experience but it is very necessary. Note how the psalmist is clear that it is God who has ordained these unpleasant experiences—'You brought us into prison. You laid burdens on our back' etc. v. 11.

Silver is refined in fire to burn out all the impurities. So God refines us in trials for the same reason. So when there are rough times do not fight against it but remember that that God chastises those whom he loves. And the purpose is always for our good—to bring us into a place of abundance (v. 12).

We need to notice the psalmist's reaction to the difficulties of vv. 10-12. He worshipped (v. 13), He was obedient to the Lord (vv. 13-14). He sought to serve the Lord (v. 15).

The Psalmist concludes with his personal testimony in verses 16-20, to answered prayer. We all ask from time to time, 'does God answer our prayers?' In many ways it is probably the greatest problem in our Christian lives. If we lose confidence in prayer it is because we have lost confidence in God, and that is deadly.

Listen to this advice on prayer. In verse 16 the psalmist addresses all who fear the Lord. In other words, those who take God seriously. The first thing about prayer is to be sure we are in a right relationship with God. If we play fast and loose with him our prayers will never be answered.

What a God we have. There is no reason for a drab and dry spiritual life. We should know the joy and excitement that the psalmist knew. And it was not the excitement of a football match or a disco, but the holy excitement of a soul in the presence of Almighty God.

On Palm Sunday as Jesus entered Jerusalem in triumph his followers were full of joy and in their excitement shouted their praise to God. The Pharisees did not like that and demanded that Jesus silence his disciples. His answer was that if he did the stones would cry out. There is a holy excitement that cannot and should not be contained. Commenting on this Calvin talked of the 'ardor which God excites'. Psalm 66 knows something of this and may we to be so moved in our day.

Psalm Seventy-Three

A LIFE BEWILDERED
BY CIRCUMSTANCES

The Psalmist in this Psalm is really bearing his soul before us, and in so doing is giving a tremendous service to the church. Here is a godly man in trouble. Something of his trouble is expressed in verse 14 but no detail is given. It may have been health difficulties, financial worries or family problems. Whatever it was it was having a profound effect upon him spiritually. He was on the brink of packing in his spiritual walk (v. 13). In effect he was saying, 'what is the use of trying to be a Christian?' He is beginning to waver (v. 2).

Have you ever felt like that? Probably most of us have at some time or other. How do we cope with such feelings? Do we bottle it all up and pretend everything is okay? Yet on the inside we are seething. Or perhaps we go to the other extreme and blurt it all out to anyone who will listen. We get so wrapped up in self-pity that we have no thought of how our doubts may affect other believers. The Psalmist was not like that—'If I had said this, I will speak thus, I would have betrayed this generation of your children.' (v. 15)

His reaction is to sit down and think. Psalm 73 is an expression of his thought process, of the stages he went through in his terrible spiritual nightmare.

What his problem was does not matter. In fact it is good that he does not exactly spell it out, because in this way the Psalm can embrace all our problems. Some Christians can cope with stress easier than others. What seems to reduce some to a blob of spiritual jelly does not bother others at all. The problem is immaterial. What is important is how we cope with these things. Never dismiss your problems as silly or think if others can cope then so should you. If your problem is causing you spiritual difficulties then it is serious and needs dealing with.

We need first of all to see that the psalmist's problem was not the prosperity of the wicked. Verses 3-12 have always been true of this sinful world. He had coped with this fact for years and would do so again in the future. He thought this was his problem but it was not.

Other people are never really our problem. They only become so when we ourselves are out of touch with God. Circumstances and events that we can take in our stride when we are spiritually healthy, floor us when we are out of fellowship with God. It may be that this problem only serves to show us that we are not as spiritually strong as we thought. It is not the problem that the spiritual affect is having on us that is the important thing.

Take for instance Paul' thorn in the flesh in 2 Corinthians 12. It could have devastated him. But he did not allow it to do so and instead it was a means of blessing. He says in verse 9, 'But he said to me, "My grace is sufficient for you, for my power is made perfect in weakness." Therefore I will boast all the more gladly about my weaknesses, so that Christ's power may rest on me. That is why for Christ's sake, I delight in weaknesses, in insults, in hardships, in persecutions, in difficulties. For when I am weak, then I am strong.'

You do not get to that point by sitting down and feeling sorry for yourself. This is the result of praying and thinking through difficulties in the light of the goodness and providence of God.

GOD IS GOOD

The first verse of this Psalm is most important as it reminds us of the never changing truth that God is good, always good, and only good to his people. Whatever we may be feeling or experiencing this is always true. If you are envying the unbelievers and thinking how much better off they are than you, it is because you have forgotten that God is good to his people. You have stopped thinking and you are reacting. A Christian should never react because it is spiritually fatal. We need to think, think and then think again.

What would you rather have, good health or a saved soul? What would you prefer, plenty of money in the bank or a spiritual inheritance? Do you really envy a man who is without Christ and therefore on his way to hell?

The key to right thinking is in verse 17. It is never an answer to a Christian's problems to stop going to church. It is there in the worship and ministry that the Psalmist begins to get things back into perspective.

The result was a deep conviction of his own sin—'When my heart was grieved and my spirit embittered, I was senseless and ignorant; I was a brute beast before you.' (vv. 21-22) Think of that, a believer acting like a beast before the God who loves him. He has been lashing out unthinkingly and trying to destroy. This is the result of the verse 13 attitude. It is a denial of divine grace and love.

It is true that his feet almost slipped (v. 2). But God is good and brings him back to see—'Yet I am always with you' (v. 23). In spite of his foolishness and bitterness, ignorance and stupid words, God is good and held him firm. There is nothing more amazing than the goodness of God. If there was a rubbish dump for spiritual failure it would be full, and heaven would be empty. Listen to the sheer wonder of verses 23-26. "Yet I am always with you; you hold me by my right hand. You guide me with your counsel, and afterwards you will take me into glory. Whom have I in heaven but you? And being with you, I desire nothing on earth. My flesh and my heart may fail, but God is the strength of my heart and my portion forever."

In spite of all the unfairness of life and the pain and anguish caused by our problems, there are still for the Christian abundant blessings now and in the future there will be glory. Why should we envy a man going to hell when there is glory awaiting us?

PRESENT BLESSINGS

Even when we are not aware of it God will never leave us or forsake us. On many occasions we could not complain if God did forsake us, but he never will. This is why even in the darkest moments, v. 15 is still true. Why did the psalmist have this spiritual sensitivity? The only answer is that even when he was behaving like a brute beast God had never left him. Often the way is dark and confusing but we are not left to work it out by ourselves. There is guidance for us (v. 24). Sometimes God guides us out of the problems, or sometimes he may show us that it is our attitude that is causing the problem. And sometimes he may say my grace is sufficient for you to cope with this. But he is always there to guide and counsel. Not only this, but God gives strength to his people (v. 26). We all know the truth of 'my flesh and my heart may fail', but God never fails. That is why Paul could say that when he was weak in his own efforts he was always strong in the Lord. Have you ever found that you are never so strong as when you are weak?

The presence of God, his guidance and strength, are the blessings we are to enjoy here and now, but the greatest blessing is expressed in verse 25—the preciousness of God himself. When we truly appreciate this everything else everything else pales into insignificance.

Psalm Eighty-One

A WORSHIPPING LIFE

Psalm 81 brings before us two quite distinct conditions of the people of God. In verses 1-7 they are enjoying God and in verses 11-16 ignoring God. Verses 8-10 are a warning and encouragement for them to move from the second condition to the first.

ENJOYING GOD

In vv. 1-7 the emphasis is on enjoying God in worship. The first three verses are a commandment on how to worship, but they are also a reflection on how Christians ought to think and behave. Here is worship full of joy and praise. But what causes them to so enjoy their worship?

It does not depend upon the instruments they were using. It would be easy to think so from the reference to the tambourine, harp and lyre. It would be a mistake to do so. These are not the essential things in worship. In the New Testament it is preaching, singing, prayer and sacraments which mark the worship of the church. Whilst singing is mentioned several times there is never any mention of instruments. New Testament worship is quite distinct from Old Testament worship. The Old Testament is essentially outward, ritualistic, depending upon objects like the altar, priests' garments, sacrifices and instruments. In the New Testament worship is spiritual with no visible altar, priest, sacrifice or instrument. It is worship in spirit and truth.

If the joy of worship depends upon visible objects there is something wrong with it. There is a particular danger concerning music. Instruments can take over, captivate and enthrall. They help whip up an atmosphere. They are alright in their place but worship does not of necessity need these things. It depends upon fellowship with God and a sense of the reality of God.

What conclusion can we draw from this?

Because New Testament worship mentions no instruments for our worship some Christians believe we should have none. Or some make a distinction between the piano and organ and all other instruments. These are permitted and others forbidden. Take for instance the organ. At the Reformation Luther used the organ, but Calvin did not regarding it as the 'pope's instrument'. When eventually it was introduced, it came with the same sort of objection as guitars and drums do today.

If the instrument is a help to worship then why not use it whether it be an organ or guitar. When it ceases to be a help and becomes essential or dominates, it is wrong. True worship does not depend upon these things but upon fellowship with God.

Do we enjoy our worship? What about our singing? In verse 1 of this psalm there is the word 'aloud'. Are we afraid of this so that we hardly open our mouths when singing? When a people are enjoying God they will inevitably enjoy singing. They look forward to their worship and it is anything but predicable.

Predictability destroys a sense of expectation, and formality can exclude any possibility of intervention by the Holy Spirit. Predictability and formality are not the same things as doing everything decently and in order. We are very conservative and feel safe with the familiar. Change disturbs us and makes us suspicious. I wonder how we would cope with revival!

IGNORING GOD

God in verses 11-16 speaks of 'my people'. They belong to God but they do not listen to him. There are inevitable consequences of this......

v. 12   God gave them over to follow their own sinful ways.
v. 14   They were subdued by their enemies.
v. 16   They were missing out on so many blessings.

I don't want to pursue these other than to ask, are they true of us? In other words which condition are we in? Are we enjoying God or ignoring him?

Perhaps our answer would be that neither is true of us. We are in between. So we are like the church in Laodicea, not hot or cold only lukewarm. If that is true surely we cannot be satisfied with this. The question we have to ask is, 'how do we get to the condition of enjoying God?' The answer is given in verse 10, 'Open wide your mouth and I will fill it.'

SPIRITUAL HUNGER

In verse 10 we see a responsibility and a promise. The responsibility is that we open wide our mouths and the promise from God is that he will fill it.

The picture here is of a fledgling in a nest with their mouths wide open to receive all the good things the parent birds have for them. It is a picture of total dependency and intense hunger. The word 'wide' suggests urgency, need and priority. There is nothing half hearted about this. The mouth is wide open to grab as much as possible and to miss nothing.

This is what we are to do before the promise will be fulfilled. Almost all the great promises of scripture are conditional (1 Chronicles 7:14; Malachi 3:10; Psalm 81:10). God is sovereign and he can work without our aid but he chooses to work through his people, so this requires them to be in earnest. He lays upon us responsibilities and demands from us obedience.

Come back to the fledgling in the nest. When the food goes into the mouth it provides nourishment, strength and health. God is promising this to us. He wants to fill us with all the things that will encourage and maintain spiritual growth. Is that what you want? Are you fed up with your own base desires? Are you weary with how sin and the world so appeal to you? When our life is saturated with God then assurance, enjoyment and satisfaction abound. It does not mean there will be no more problems but v. 14 will then become a reality.

There is so much for us in Christ, so why do we live on bread and water when there is a banqueting table available. How do we open our mouths wide? By using the means of grace—prayer, the Bible and fellowship. We need to stop waiting for something to happen and instead take the initiative in response to God's promise.

Psalm Ninety-Six

A PRACTICAL LIFE

The psalmist is encouraging us to delight in the Lord. The reason we should do so is spelt out very clearly in vv. 4-6. God is great and there is no one like him. No believer would argue with that but how do we ascribe or give to the Lord the glory due to his name?

Our text tells us two practical ways to do this—worship and offering.

WORSHIP

What is worship? *'Worship is to feel in the heart a humbling but delightful sense of admiring awe and astonished wonder, and to express it in some appropriate manner. Worship is awesome wonder and overpowering love in the presence of God'.* - A. W. Tozer

If worship is such a great privilege, it stands to reason that one of the first things you need to do after conversion is to learn to worship God.

We're here to be worshippers first and workers only second. We take a convert and immediately make a worker out of him. God never meant it to be so. God meant that a convert should learn to be a worshipper, and after that he can learn to be a worker.

A certain degree of worship will come automatically. You will praise and worship God for what he has done for you. But worship is more than that. Read Tozer's definition again, 'admiring awe and astonished wonder'. In other words, when we realize how great and holy our God is, there comes over us a tremendous sense of awe and wonder. We then worship God not merely for what he has done for us, but for who he is and what he is. The more you know of God, the more you will worship God. The more you know God, the more you will love God, and love is the true basis of worship: 'Thou shalt love the Lord thy God with all thy heart, and with all thy soul, and with all thy might' (Deuteronomy 6:5 A V).

It is quite impossible to worship God without loving Him. Scripture and reason agree to declare this. And God is never satisfied with anything less than all: 'all thy heart ... all thy soul ... , all thy might'.

To hear some Christians talk you would think there are two parts of a service—sermon and worship. But that is wrong. The whole service is worship.

It is sometimes objected that in most churches the congregation does not fully enter into worship, and that what we need is more participation by the whole church. To say this is to fail to understand that in singing, praying, preaching and hearing, every person present should be actively engaged. This is obvious when we are all singing, but the same is true about the prayer and the sermon. One person will lead in prayer, but all should be praying; and you will already have discovered that there is no greater stimulant to worship than biblical preaching in the power of the Spirit. The preacher says something that causes your heart to praise and adore your Savior. He is preaching; you are listening; but you are both worshipping.

We now come to the ticklish question. If worship is such a great privilege, why is that many, one could argue most, Christians, are content to attend only one service on Sunday. They are there in the morning but rarely if ever in the evening.

Forget for the moment families with young children and one parent is baby sitting in the evening; forget also those who because of age or health can only come once. Let's focus on the believer who could be there in the evening but stays away. Why?

He may argue, the Bible says nothing about two services on Sunday so there is no obligation. But we are not talking about obligation but delight. Why does he not delight to have as much of the privilege as possible? Is it that the one-cer has other symptoms as well—he rarely attends a midweek meeting; he does not pray and read the Bible every day.

The sad fact is that far too many church people today are only playing at being Christians. For them Christianity is a hobby. There is no commitment or enthusiasm for the work of the gospel.

If you think I am being too hard, just take a look at the state of the church today. It is self evident that something is radically wrong.

Or take an honest look at your own heart. Are you a believer who after 5 or 10 years of being in the faith are still a spiritual infant? There has been no spiritual growth. Are you happy with that? Then what are you going to do about it? Read Hebrews 5: 11-14

There are three remedies given ...

5: 14 train yourself
6: 11 be diligent
6:12 do not be lazy.

Let's go back for a moment to a word we used a few minutes ago: obligation. Here is a word not liked by many Christians. But let me give you an example where obligation is crucial.

Baptism. The Bible knows nothing of unbaptised believers. There may be a dispute over the mode but not the act. When Jesus said, "Repent, Believe and be Baptised", he was not making a suggestion. He was laying before us an obligation.

OFFERING

Years ago there was a popular song which ran 'Money is the root of all evil'. Like so many popular things in the world, the song was wrong. The Bible says, 'For the love of money is a root of all kinds of evil' (1 Timothy 6:10). Money is neither good nor bad in itself. It is man's attitude to it that causes trouble.

What should be the Christian's attitude to money? We should certainly not love money. Neither should we regard money as evil. Without it the church could not maintain its ministry and its missionary work. The Bible teaches us that we are stewards of all God has given us, including our money. Whether we have a lot or a little, it is to be used wisely for the glory of God. It needs to be stressed that whether we are rich or poor, we are stewards of what we have, and the Bible's teaching on the use of money covers the conditions of poverty and of wealth.

How should we use our money? It is to be used to provide the necessities of life for ourselves and for our family (housing, clothing, food, etc.). This is a duty laid upon us in the Word of God (1 Timothy 5:8). Money is to be used also for pleasure and recreation (books, holidays, etc.). It is God's will that we enjoy this beautiful world which he has made, but the Christian must be careful not to waste his money on the passing fancies of the world.

The Bible makes it clear, however, that the Christian is a person who gives money away, and who does so not now and again grudgingly, but regularly and cheerfully (2 Corinthians 9:7). This giving is done generally in three directions: (a) to our local church; (b) to a missionary work; (c) to a charity. Very often money given to the local church covers these three aspects of giving, as the church both uses and distributes the money received. Another way of giving, which is a beautiful expression of Christian love, is what the Authorized Version of the Bible calls 'almsgiving' (Luke 12:33; Acts 9:36; 10:2). This is when you see an individual or a family in need, 16:1-3; and without any fuss (Matthew 6:1-4) you help with a gift. All giving produces a sense of joy in the giver (Acts 20:35), but almsgiving is particularly satisfying.

TITHING?

The question that bothers many is, 'How much should I give?' The basis of the Old Testament teaching was tithing. Read

Leviticus 27:30-33; Deuteronomy 12:6-18; 14:22-29; 2 Chronicles 31:5; Nehemiah 10:37. Basically this meant that one tenth of a person's income was given to the Lord. In the New Testament, tithing is nowhere commanded as a requirement for the Christian. There is a great emphasis upon giving, but not on tithing. However, this does not mean that tithing has no bearing upon the Christian's life. If, before Christ came, God's people gave one-tenth of their income to the Lord, should it be any less for those of us who have known the full revelation of the love of God in Jesus Christ? Clearly it should be more.

All your money is God's. One-tenth is a good place to start giving to the Lord. But our giving is not to be legalistic, but spiritual. We give not because, we must, but because we love and are loved. We are to give out of the prosperity the Lord has given us (1 Corinthians 16:2).

Notice how the apostle Paul, when he is dealing with the question of giving money to others, introduces two remarkable descriptions of God's great gift to us: 'For you know the grace of our Lord Jesus Christ, that though he was rich, yet for your sakes he became poor, so that you through his poverty might become rich' (2 Corinthians 8:9); and 'Thanks be to God for his indescribable gift!' (2 Corinthians 9: 15).

This is the way we are to give, with our hearts filled with the knowledge of God's love to us, and of how much we owe him. Our giving is a response to God's giving: 'Freely you have received, freely give' (Matthew 10:8).

You can only give your money to God as an act of worship in this way if you have first given yourself (2 Corinthians 8:5).

Psalm One Hundred-Three

A LIFE IN STEP WITH GOD

Why should a man want to praise the Lord? The simple fact is that most don't. They don't see that they have anything to praise the Lord for. So why is David so absorbed in praising God? The only reason a man will praise the Lord is if he sees he has good reason to do so. David tells us his reason in verse 3—"He forgives all my sins".

The praise is not produced by a man's position in life, or intellect, or material prosperity, but it is a spiritual appreciation. Notice in verse 1 that David calls upon his soul to praise. The soul is that which distinguishes man from all other created beings. It is the life of God in man. Yet it is a soul in bondage to sin. A soul dead in sin, and further, it is an immortal soul.

Man's body may suffer but death will end that, but his soul is immortal. Death cannot touch it therefore the corruption and damnation of sin will last forever. Once a man realizes this basic truth about himself, he will groan with deep anguish. To realize he has on immortal soul that is damned to hell for all eternity because of his sin is a terrifying prospect. It therefore becomes clear that the salvation of his soul is crucial. If a man's sin is forgiven then his soul is saved. If his soul is spared hell and set for heaven then he cannot but praise the Lord.

The little word *all* in verse 3 is important. If you were to ask how much sin does it take to damn a soul to hell? The Bible would answer only one. "For whoever keeps the whole law, and yet stumbles at just one point, is guilty of breaking all of it". (James 2:10). We may bluster with indignation at that and deem it unfair, but that is the way it is. Sin is to break God's law and God's law is one entity not a collection of many. So to break what we call one, is to break it all. But it does not matter how little or large our sin is, God forgives ALL sin. He leaves no trace; leaves no guilt that could condemn us.

To have some sins forgiven and others not would be of no help to guilty souls. It would leave our condemnation unchanged. But to know that all sin is forgiven prompts great praise for the Lord.

The thrill of the Christian gospel is that it offers a full and complete pardon for every sin. John delights to tell us that 'the blood of Jesus his son, purifies us from all sin' (1 John 1:7). All means every sin with no exception. This does not mean that God treats sin as unimportant and of no consequence. Forgiveness is not cheap and easy. On the contrary the whole Bible speaks of the vileness and horror of sin. Forgiveness is not a simple exercise. David alludes to this in verse 10. Stop and think about it. Sin is against God's love, compassion and goodness. It contaminates his glorious creation and it can never live at peace with God. Hell is not only its just reward, it is the only place sin can go.

That such sin should be forgiven is cause for praising God. Can you praise God because he has forgiven all your sin?

But the Christian does not just praise God that his sin is forgiven, he praises God because of who he is. God is always the same and men ought always to praise him, but they don't. It is this whole question of sins forgiven that instigates praise.

WHY ARE MY SINS FORGIVEN?

Why does not God treat me as I deserve? (v. 10). The answer is found in the character of God in verse 8. Who can describe the mercy and love of God? David tries to in verse 11, but even this is inadequate to describe a love that is as great and immense as God himself. In verse 17 David is caught in the same dilemma. What is divine love and mercy like? It is from everlasting to everlasting. It is as high as heaven. Language fails. Words and concepts are inadequate. All you can say is, 'Praise the Lord, O my soul.'

That God should love such guilty sinners as us is truly amazing. That God should pay such a price as the death of his son to make salvation possible is incredible. But this is the heart and glory of the gospel. If we had but a shred of understanding of the depth and depravity of our sin in the sight of the holy God, we could not help but Praise the Lord.

Think for a moment what it means to have *all* your sins forgiven. David says in verse 5 that it is like having your youth renewed. It is like having a fresh start; like being born again. Of course the words 'born again' come from Jesus. He said unless we are born again we cannot enter heaven. This is because no sin will be allowed to enter heaven. Therefore we must get *all* our sins forgiven, and forgiveness is preceded by the new birth.

In sin we are dead to God with no spiritual awareness and no desire for God. We are dead and helpless. Then the Holy Spirit awakens us. We hear what God is saying. At first we don't like the accusation of sin. We resent it but the Holy Spirit will not let it go until we believe. Then we groan over our sin because we become aware of the bondage we are in to sin. We see that death and hell are awaiting us. We are under conviction of sin. Our greatest desire is to have forgiveness and salvation.

David did not know it when he wrote this psalm but all the mercies of God come to us via the Lord Jesus Christ. Forgiveness is possible because Jesus took the punishment our sin deserved. Because of this God removes our sin "as far as the east is from the west..." (v. 12). In the words of Sir Richard Baker, commenting on these verses: "Why is it that God hath not dealt with us after our sins? Is it not because he hath dealt with another after our sins? Another who took our sins upon him...O gracious God, thou art too just to take revenge twice for the same faults; and therefore, having turned thy fierce wrath upon him, thou wilt not turn it upon us too; but having rewarded him according to our iniquities, thou wilt now reward us according to his merits."

David calls upon his soul not to forget all God's benefits to us. These benefits of grace are the reason to praise the Lord.

Psalm One Hundred-Nineteen

A LIFE GROUNDED
IN THE WORD OF GOD

Every Christian knows Psalm 119 as the longest chapter in the Bible with its 176 verses. But it is far more than that and is probably the most carefully constructed chapter in the Bible. It has 22 parts, with each part prefixed with the subtitle of a letter from the Hebrew alphabet. Each part has 8 verses beginning with the same letter of the subtitle.

The psalmist here demonstrates his great love for the word of God and almost every verse has a direct reference to the scriptures. It may be called the word or law or commands or precepts or statutes or decrees, but it is clear what he is talking about. In verse 57 he says, 'You are my portion , O Lord, I have promised to obey your words.' This psalm has been a great help to Christians down through the ages. In the 18th century Henry Vine said, 'This is the psalm I often had recourse to when I could find no spirit of prayer in my own heart, and at length the fire was kindled and I could pray.' The great missionary Henry Martyn said, 'My heart was beginning to sink into discontent at my unprofitableness but by reading some of Psalm 119 and prayer, I recovered.'

If the Lord is to be our portion, our joy and delight, then the word must be central to our thinking and living. Psalm 119 shows us that there is no point in our lives and no situation that can confront us where God's word does not minister to our needs.

YOUNG CHRISTIAN v. 9

Every young Christian knows the significance of the question voiced in verse 9. Pressures, temptations and natural desires all work to pollute the mind and pull the young believer from the path of righteousness. The answer to this is give serious attention to all that is written in God's word.

This advice is repeated by Peter, 'Like newborn babies, crave pure spiritual milk, so that by it you may grow up in your salvation' (1 Peter 2:2). God's word is food for the soul and without it there is no growth. And growth means strength and maturity. Every young believer needs to treasure the Bible and listen intently as it is taught.

OLDER CHRISTIAN vv. 93,97

The Christian never grows out of a need of scripture. Read verses 93 and 97, 'I will never forget your precepts, for by them you have renewed my life...Oh, how I love your law! I meditate on it all day long.' These can only be the words of an older saint. It is experience speaking. Here we see indebtedness—'I will never forget.' We see passion—'Oh how I love your law.' These things belong to a child of God who has proved in all the joys and problems of life the value of God's word.

Look now at some of his experiences.

COMFORT vv. 25,28,50,52,165

How does the word of God bring comfort to the Christian?

This is clearly seen in Luke 24 and the story of the road to Emmaus. We see from v. 17 that Cleopas and his friend were downcast. Jesus could have changed that in a moment by revealing himself to them, but instead they were kept from recognizing him. Instead Jesus turns them to the Scriptures (vv. 26-27). The Scripture puts their sadness into the context of God's sovereign purpose. The effect of this is, 'were not our hearts burning within us while he talked with us on the road and opened the Scriptures to us.' Their hearts were burning before their eyes were opened.

Scripture shows us who God is and reveals to us his ways. This is a great source of comfort.

TRIALS vv. 95,107,143

In trials we must learn to flee to the word of God. So many believers make the fatal mistake in trials of feeling sorry for themselves and blaming God. They then neglect worship, prayer and scripture. That is Satan's leading.

In trials follow the psalmist's advice, 'Trouble and distress have come upon me, but you're your commands are my delight' (v. 143). Now see how this works out in practice in Jeremiah 20. We see the trial in v. 2. Then in v. 7 the prophet begins to falter. He blames God in v. 8 and determines to pack it all in (v. 9). He would have done this but "his word is in my heart like a fire". This alone keeps the man of God and soon leads to the triumph of verses 11 and 13.

11 But the LORD is with me like a mighty warrior;
so my persecutors will stumble and not prevail.
They will fail and be thoroughly disgraced;
their dishonor will never be forgotten.
13 Sing to the LORD!
Give praise to the LORD!
He rescues the life of the needy
from the hands of the wicked.

REBUKES   vv. 71,75

There are times when the Christian is not being wronged but is wrong. It is the scriptures that God uses to show him this and put him right. This starts with rebuke (v. 71). James says that the Bible is like a mirror. When we look into it, it shows us what we are. We see this illustrated in the life of Josiah on 2 Chronicles 34. The King is earnest and sincere in wanting to do the right thing (verses 3 and 8), but even then he was ignorant of God's ways. Then in verse 15 he finds the Book. He reads it and the result we see in verse 19. He is severely rebuked.

Praise God for such an effect of Scripture. It brings us back to the Lord. As Psalm 119:57 tells us the only way to have a profitable experience of God is by being obedient to his word.

GUIDANCE   vv. 59 and 105

The Bible is our rule book. We seem to have so much trouble with guidance but our answer is to stick to biblical paths. The Bible lays down broad guidelines. It will not tell us which house to buy or who to marry. But if we follow the guidelines even these things become clear. Our trouble is that we seem to ignore the general and want instead the specific. We always seem to be looking for the extraordinary and treat the Bible like a lucky dip. Listen to 2 Peter 1:19-21, 'And we have the word of the prophets made more certain, and you will do well to pay attention to it, as to a light shining in a dark place, until the day dawns and the morning star rises in your hearts. Above all, you must understand that no prophecy of Scripture came about by the prophet's own interpretation. For prophecy never had its origin in the will of man, but men spoke from God as they were carried along by the Holy Spirit.'

Joshua is a good example of this. God performed many remarkable miracles for him but these were not to be his guidelines. 'Be strong and very courageous. Be careful to obey all the law my servant Moses gave you; do not turn from it to the right or to the left, that you may be successful wherever you go. Do not let this Book of the Law depart from your mouth; meditate on it day and night, so that you may be careful to do everything written in it. Then you will be prosperous and successful' (Joshua 1:7-8).

The Bible is crucial to our daily living. 'Your word is a lamp to my feed, and a light for my path' (Psalm 119:105).

HOLINESS vv. 7,101,128

Holiness is not some vague blessing which suddenly comes to a believer. It is a direct result of living in obedience to scripture. We are to be holy not wait to be made holy.

Here then is the value of this glorious, infallible, inspired word of God. May we, like the psalmist, be people of the Book.

Psalm One Hundred-Thirty

A PENITENT LIFE

This psalm is known as one of the great penitent psalms. It expresses the feelings of a man who desperately wants to be right with God. Every Christian has known the feelings expressed here both before and after conversion. We are going to consider it from the position of a man before he is saved.

It divides itself easily into four parts.

His problem— 1-2   His hope— 3-4

His action—   5-6   His confidence— 7-8

HIS PROBLEM vv. 1-2

Here is a man in the depths of despair. He feels as if he is in a deep hole with steep, unclimbable sides. Many problems could make us feel like this—family worries, poor health, financial concerns. But these are not the issues in the psalm. The depths here, as is obvious from the context, is conviction of his own personal sin and guilt. He does not want money, he wants mercy.

Most people never seem to see sin as a problem, and that is because life is lived with no thought of God. Or if God is thought of it is a totally false view of God. That is why people say I don't like preaching about sin. It makes me feel uncomfortable and miserable, and I don't go to church to feel miserable. This attitude never sees God as holy and righteous, but only as a celestial Santa Claus who exists to make us feel good.

How different from the psalmist. Twice times in the first two verses he cries to the Lord. The more he sees God, the more he feels the depth of his sin. The more he sees his sin, the more he cries to the Lord. Have you ever felt like this? Do you know what you are in the sight of the holy God? If God were to say to you, ask of me one thing, anything. Would you ask for mercy?

HIS CONFIDENCE vv. 3-4

The depth of sin which this man feels tends to destroy all confidence. It creates the cry of Romans 7, 'O wretched man that I am.' That is anything but confidence, and rightly so.

When someone comes under conviction it shows him his helplessness and hopelessness. There is nothing he can do, no more than a leopard can change his spots. An awareness of sin destroys self confidence, but that does not mean it leaves a sinner with no confidence. His confidence is in God.

This confidence is expressed beautifully in vv. 3-4 and is based on the fact that only God can deal with our sin. God does keep a record of sin and reminds the sinner he will one day have to stand before God and be answerable for every sin he ever committed. But this record is not irrevocable. It can be destroyed; the dept can be fully paid; the slate wiped clean. That is the confidence that the gospel gives. There is forgiveness with God.

Listen to the promises of God,

Ps 103:12.   He will remove our sins as far as the east is from the west

Heb 8:12   He will remember our sin no more

Romans 8:1 There is no condemnation to those in Christ.

All this is possible because of what God did for us in Christ. This confidence does not lead a man to trifle with God and think that sin is does not matter. On the contrary the psalmist says in v. 3 'therefore you are feared.' The wonder and amazement of forgiveness of sin causes the sinner to begin to take God seriously. Are you beginning to think of God like this?

HIS ACTION vv. 5-6

If you are beginning to have this confidence in the mercy and forgiveness of God, what should you do? The answer is in verses 5-6. We are told to wait for the Lord. Wait does not mean to sit down and do nothing. It is not a spiritual fatalism. It means to trust the Lord and seek the forgiveness which he promises. We are reminded of two things here that the seeking soul needs to know.

Firstly, your action of seeing God is based on the promises of God's word. It is not just some fancy or imagination of your mind. Your hope is in God's word. This makes very serious statements to men and women. The basic message of the Bible can be read in John 3:16 and again in Acts 4:12. The seeker needs Jesus. He is the only Savior. 'And this is the testimony: God has given us eternal life, and this life is in his Son. He who has the Son has life; he who does not have the Son of God does not have life.' (1 John 5).

Secondly, in v. 6 we see the intensity of the seeking. This is no passing whim. Have you ever lay awake at night and can't sleep. You toss and turn; look at the clock but it hardly seems to move. More than anything you want morning to come, but it never seems to come.

This is something of the intensity that the sinner ought to have in seeking God. Nothing is more important and nothing more urgent.

You want to be saved. You need to be saved. You must be saved. And your prayer is that God would save you now!

HIS HOPE vv. 7-8

The sinner's only hope is in the unfailing love of God.

Human love can fail because its source is unstable and often its motives are not pure and selfless. God's love is different. It flows from the heart of God; the heart that knows no sin or impure motives. It is as unchanging as the character of God. His love can no more change that his holiness can. It is a love that is not empty sentiment but erupts in the most wonderful of all ways at the cross.

If God has already given Jesus to die for you, you can guarantee it will never fail you. This is reinforced in the words 'full redemption' in v. 7. Redemption means to be set free from the bondage of sin by the payment of a ransom price. The problem of sin puts us in slavery to sin. Jesus is the Redeemer who pays the ransom price to set us free.

- It is a full redemption because of the price that was paid... the death of Jesus.
- It is a full redemption because of the promise of Jesus...I give them eternal life and they shall never perish.
- It is a full redemption because the gifts of God are irrevocable; they can never be taken back.

A full redemption means once saved, always saved, because all sin, past, present and future, has been dealt with. This is the sinners hope: 'God himself will redeem us.'

Psalm One Hundred-Fifty

A LIFE OF PRAISE

This is a fitting end to this remarkable collection of psalms. Several men contributed to the writing of these psalms, but almost any of them could have written 150 because it sums up their attitude to God. The psalms cover almost all the different circumstances of life from joy to despair. They show the man of God in all the varied responses to these circumstances, but the overriding reaction to them all is praise.

Whether it is the trouble of Psalm 3, the difficulties of 59 or the stress of 63, there is always reason to praise the Lord. Such praise is no mere glib mouthing of words but the genuine reflection of a heart that knows the reality of God and has learnt to trust him in all circumstances.

Take for instance Asaph in Psalm 73. His problems are very real. His heart was grieved and his spirit embittered (v. 21). He felt like a brute beast before God (v. 22). Spiritually speaking he had almost gone and lost his way altogether (v. 2). It is difficult to imagine a worse case of a believer in distress, yet he is still able to say that God is good (v. 1).

No one wants trouble and Asaph certainly did not want to go through what he was experiencing. If he could have he would have avoided the problems, but even in them he knew that God was with him. This surely is cause for praise.

As we have already seen even when we are not aware of it God will never leave us or forsake us. On many occasions we could not complain if God did forsake us, but he never will. This is why that even in the darkest moments, v. 15 is still true. Why did the psalmist have this spiritual sensitivity? The only answer is that even when he was behaving like a brute beast God had never left him. Often the way is dark and confusing but we are not left to work it out by ourselves.

There is guidance for us (v. 24). Sometimes God guides us out of the problems, or sometimes he may show us that it is our attitude that is causing the problem. And sometimes he may say 'my grace is sufficient for you' to cope with this. But he is always there to guide and counsel. Not only this, but God gives strength to his people (v. 26). We all know the truth of 'my flesh and my heart may fail', but God never fails. That is why Paul could say that when he was weak in his own efforts he was always strong in the Lord (2 Cor. 12:9,10). Have you ever found that you are never so strong as when you are weak? This is because you have found all your strength in him.

The presence of God, his guidance and strength, are the blessings we are to enjoy here and now, but the greatest blessing is expressed in verse 25—the preciousness of God himself. When we truly appreciate this, then everything else pales into insignificance.

The final psalm begins and ends with a royal command that is always fitting: *Praise the LORD!* Will you obey? Well, will you?

OTHER SOLID GROUND TITLES

We recently celebrated our tenth anniversary of uncovering buried treasure to the glory of God. During these ten years we have produced over 320 volumes. A sample is listed below:

Biblical & Theological Studies: *Addresses to Commemorate the 100th Anniversary of Princeton Theological Seminary in 1912* by Allis, Machen, Wilson, Vos, Warfield and many more.

Notes on Galatians by J. Gresham Machen

The Origin of Paul's Religion by J. Gresham Machen

A Scientific Investigation of the Old Testament by R.D. Wilson

Theology on Fire: *Sermons from Joseph A. Alexander*

Evangelical Truth: *Sermons for the Family* by Archibald Alexander

A Shepherd's Heart: *Pastoral Sermons of James W. Alexander*

Grace & Glory: *Sermons from Princeton Chapel* by Geerhardus Vos

The Lord of Glory by Benjamin B. Warfield

The Person & Work of the Holy Spirit by Benjamin B. Warfield

The Power of God unto Salvation by Benjamin B. Warfield

Calvin Memorial Addresses by Warfield, Johnson, Orr, Webb...

The Five Points of Calvinism by Robert Lewis Dabney

Annals of the American Presbyterian Pulpit by W.B. Sprague

The Word & Prayer: *Classic Devotions from the Pen of John Calvin*

A Body of Divinity: *Sum and Substance of Christian Doctrine* by Ussher

The Complete Works of Thomas Manton

A Puritan New Testament Commentary by John Trapp

Exposition of the Epistle to the Hebrews by William Gouge

Exposition of the Epistle of Jude by William Jenkyn

Lectures on the Book of Esther by Thomas M'Crie

Lectures on the Book of Acts by John Dick

To order any of our titles please contact us in one of three ways:

Call us at **1-205-443-0311**
Email us at **mike.sgcb@gmail.com**
Visit our website at **www.solid-ground-books.com**

CPSIA information can be obtained at www.ICGtesting.com
Printed in the USA
LVOW061308200112

264813LV00002B/4/P